GLOBAL THINKERS
AND DOERS SINCE 1911

Printed in USA by RR Donnelley
Author: Dave Whitaker
Design: Pivot Design, Inc.
www.pivotdesign.com

FIRST EDITION

Published by Uppercase Books, Inc.
33 W Erie St Chicago, IL 60654

GLOBAL THINKERS AND DOERS SINCE 1911

While The Executives' Club of Chicago is often recognized for the prominence of its speakers, The Club's leaders have long recognized that its members are the lifeblood of the organization.

43

INTRODUCTION:
A CENTURY TO CELEBRATE

For The Executives' Club of Chicago, 2011 was a year to celebrate and invigorate, reaffirm and renew. As one of the nation's oldest and most prestigious business organizations, The Executives' Club commemorated its centennial anniversary by building on its proud tradition of service to generations of Chicago's global thinkers and doers.

Founded in 1911, The Club of today reflects the evolution of the city that inspired its beginnings. With thought leadership, professional development and effective business practices forming the core of its programming, it is a forum that provides its members with the information and resources needed to establish effective global partnerships, enhance intellectual exchange, develop future diverse business leaders, and promote Chicago as a world class global business center.

It is from these unified tenets that The Club designed a Centennial Celebration filling its milestone year with dynamic programming events and activities punctuated by four Centennial Summits—addressing women's leadership, technology leadership, new leaders, and U.S.-India trade and investment relations. As an organization that presents more than 60 distinguished programs each year, the special gatherings and keynote addresses of its centennial season offer only a hint of the supportive role this powerhouse business forum has played in the life of Chicago business and beyond.

An added element of its Centennial Celebration, this exclusive anniversary book recognizes a commitment to progress that stretches back 100 years. While capturing the programming highlights and festive nature of its centennial year, this book also revisits the richness of The Club's past. Through historical accounts and illustrations culled from the organization's archives, the pages ahead revive the voices of notable figures from the worlds of business, finance, politics and academia and trace The Club's generational growth and enduring impact on the business culture of Chicago.

In bringing its heritage forward, the prominent leaders, thinkers, and speakers who propelled The Club's influential rise over many decades are integrated with the perspectives of those who continue to contribute to its success.

For more than 60 years, The Executives' Club of Chicago held most of its speakers' luncheons and other special events at the Hotel Sherman. At various points in its long life, the hotel was among the most recognizable in the city. It was closed in 1973 and was demolished in 1980. The site is now occupied by the Thompson Center, formerly the State of Illinois Center.

The book also features Heritage Profiles of organizations that serve as key partners in The Club's mission to share effective business practices and advance Chicago's role as a leading business center.

In telling the story of The Executives' Club of Chicago, this book follows the path of the organization's accomplishments as well as the challenges that sharpened its ability to adapt to new eras and changing needs. But, ultimately, it tells the story of a community coming together.

Whether presenting a panel of experts, facilitating intellectual exchange, offering unparalleled opportunities for young leaders to enhance their business acumen or encouraging corporate partnerships that lead to innovative achievements in the global marketplace, the principles of The Club's programming have always been inspired by the people of Chicago and the power of collective pursuits. In its centennial year, The Executives' Club of Chicago celebrated its history of bringing people together with the same spirit of community that guided its past, and a sense of purpose to carry its lasting legacy well into the future.

SUMMARIZING THE SCOPE OF THE EXECUTIVES' CLUB OF CHICAGO

The Executives' Club's signature programs, along with added calendar meetings and receptions, deliver a combined portfolio of approximately 60 public and private events each year. Presenting influential global leaders of forward thinking, highly competitive companies and organizations that evidence innovation and excellence, the chosen topics of its programs reflect current business and economic trends, both domestic and global, and respond to the expressed needs of The Club's membership.

By meeting these parameters, The Executives' Club's gatherings give new meaning to the term, "thought leadership," and provide invaluable support to Chicago's development as a global business center. Most programs are open to the public, with members of The Club receiving significant discounts as a benefit of membership.

GLOBAL LEADERS LUNCHEONS

One of the nation's premier speakers forums, The Executives' Club's Global Leaders Luncheons provide members and guests with unprecedented access to the political, policy, corporate, and institutional leaders whose expertise, insights, and experience shape the global business climate. Held September through June, and many in conjunction with one of The Club's active committees, these enlightening luncheons target a diverse range of industries and explore topics chosen for their relevance to current global business and economic trends. Drawing from Chicagoland's C-suite executives, senior professionals and emerging leaders, Global Leaders Luncheons consistently attract audiences of 800–1,000.

CHICAGO CEO BREAKFASTS

At quarterly breakfasts, The Executives' Club introduces the Chicago business community to CEOs who have recently taken the helm of multinational corporations headquartered in the metropolitan area, who have recently relocated their companies to the city or whose organizations have unique stories, strategies or successes to share with Chicago's business leaders. Chicago CEO Breakfasts not only showcase the innovative strategies these talented CEOs rely on to remain competitive, they also help build and maintain a sense of community, even as that community grows and changes.

TECHNOLOGY CONFERENCES

The Executives' Club's quarterly Technology Conferences bring together leaders of established companies and start-ups to address technology strategy, innovation, return on investment, outsourcing, and security, with particular emphasis on leveraging technology to revitalize the regional economy. The conferences present interactive panels of Chief Technology Officers (CTOs) and Chief Information Officers (CIOs), CEOs of emerging technology ventures, and senior IT consultants. Each fall conference is highlighted by the presentation of the CIO of the Year Award, conferred jointly by The Executives' Club and the Association of Information Technology Professionals to honor CIOs whose exceptional leadership drives business value, enhances customer service, builds business partnerships, and improves organizational effectiveness.

WOMEN'S LEADERSHIP BREAKFASTS

Launched in 2004, The Executives' Club's quarterly Women's Leadership Breakfasts have become one of the nation's largest speakers' forum dedicated to the needs and interests of business and professional women. These breakfast programs regularly attract more than 1000 attendees, primarily women, for programs featuring remarkable women who are role models of success. Each breakfast is organized around a theme relevant to women from diverse fields—such as how women are redefining leadership, the importance of establishing a personal brand, and the role of social responsibility and community service. Speakers are selected for their capacity to impart lessons of value to women at varying stages in their careers.

NEW LEADERS CIRCLE

The Executives' Club of Chicago's New Leaders Circle helps prepare a new generation of young, diverse, global and civic-minded thought leaders for Chicagoland corporations and institutions. Designed to serve Club members 40 years old or younger who demonstrate leadership qualities and are on a fast track career path, the New Leaders Circle cultivates emerging leaders through leadership development programs and a unique group mentoring program that provide extraordinary access to Chicago's senior executives and promote a sense of community among the future leaders of the region's future economy. In addition to providing leadership opportunities to its membership, the New Leaders Circle Advisory Board provides strategic direction to all programs of The Club that serve aspiring leaders.

SPECIAL PROGRAMMING

In response to the rapid pace of change in the political, economic, industrial, and commercial landscape, The Executives' Club periodically hosts programs that focus on specific issues, regions, and populations driving these changes, or feature prominent thought leaders, including heads of state, authors, and other public figures. Past forums have addressed global sustainability, health care reform, and U.S. trade relations with the European Union and Mercosur nations.

The Club also hosts evening receptions to welcome new members and to thank existing members, Directors and Committee Chairs, as well as provide networking opportunities for members and their guests. These receptions are sponsored by The Club's Board of Directors with support from leading Chicagoland businesses.

LEADERSHIP

Throughout its history, The Executives' Club of Chicago has been fortunate to have an active and engaged Board of Directors. Reflecting Chicago's standing as a global business hub, the Board is comprised of CEOs and leaders from among the top global companies headquartered in the Chicago area.

COMMITTEES

The Executives' Club's industry and civic committees help connect members with the people and issues most influential to their businesses. Each committee is led by Co-Chairs representing Chicago's who's who in industry leadership. These leaders develop and advance committee-initiated thought leadership programs where local, national, and global industry leaders explore cutting edge issues and where members can network with others who share their special interests.

More than 1,000 members participate in committee meetings and briefings held throughout the season. Serving on a committee is a membership benefit of The Club and provides members with an opportunity to become actively engaged in Club and civic initiatives.

MEMBERSHIP

The Club's membership includes leaders from 25 major industry sectors—from finance, healthcare, law, and insurance to technology, manufacturing, real estate, and retail. Other members are professionals from Midwest philanthropic institutions, universities and colleges, and state and national governments. The Club's membership also includes representatives of the international diplomatic community.

Membership to The Club is by invitation only, with new members nominated by current members. Members are nominated to and accepted by The Executives' Club of Chicago without regard to gender, race, religion or age.

OFFICE OF THE MAYOR
CITY OF CHICAGO
RAHM EMANUEL, MAYOR

January 9, 2012

Dear Friends and Members of The Executives' Club of Chicago:

As Mayor and on behalf of the City of Chicago, I offer my warmest greetings to the members of The Executives' Club of Chicago and congratulate you on 100 years of success in bringing together leaders from our business community to encourage the debate and development of business practices for the future.

Throughout its 100 years, The Executives' Club of Chicago has consistently enhanced the exchange of ideas and encouraged the development of business leaders in Chicago. Each year, The Club presents invaluable forums for the world's most influential thinkers to convene and share ideas to address the needs of our economy and our future. Chicago is fortunate to be home to such a dynamic collection of the business community's most innovative and progressive minds.

I look forward to working together to invest in our future so that we can create a strong and resilient economy which not only benefits the residents of our great city, but contributes to the continued growth and development of our nation.

I applaud The Executives' Club of Chicago for the vision and tenacity with which it has turned ideas into reality and strengthened our city and nation. Congratulations on 100 years of success and may you see 100 more.

Sincerely,

Mayor
Chicago, IL

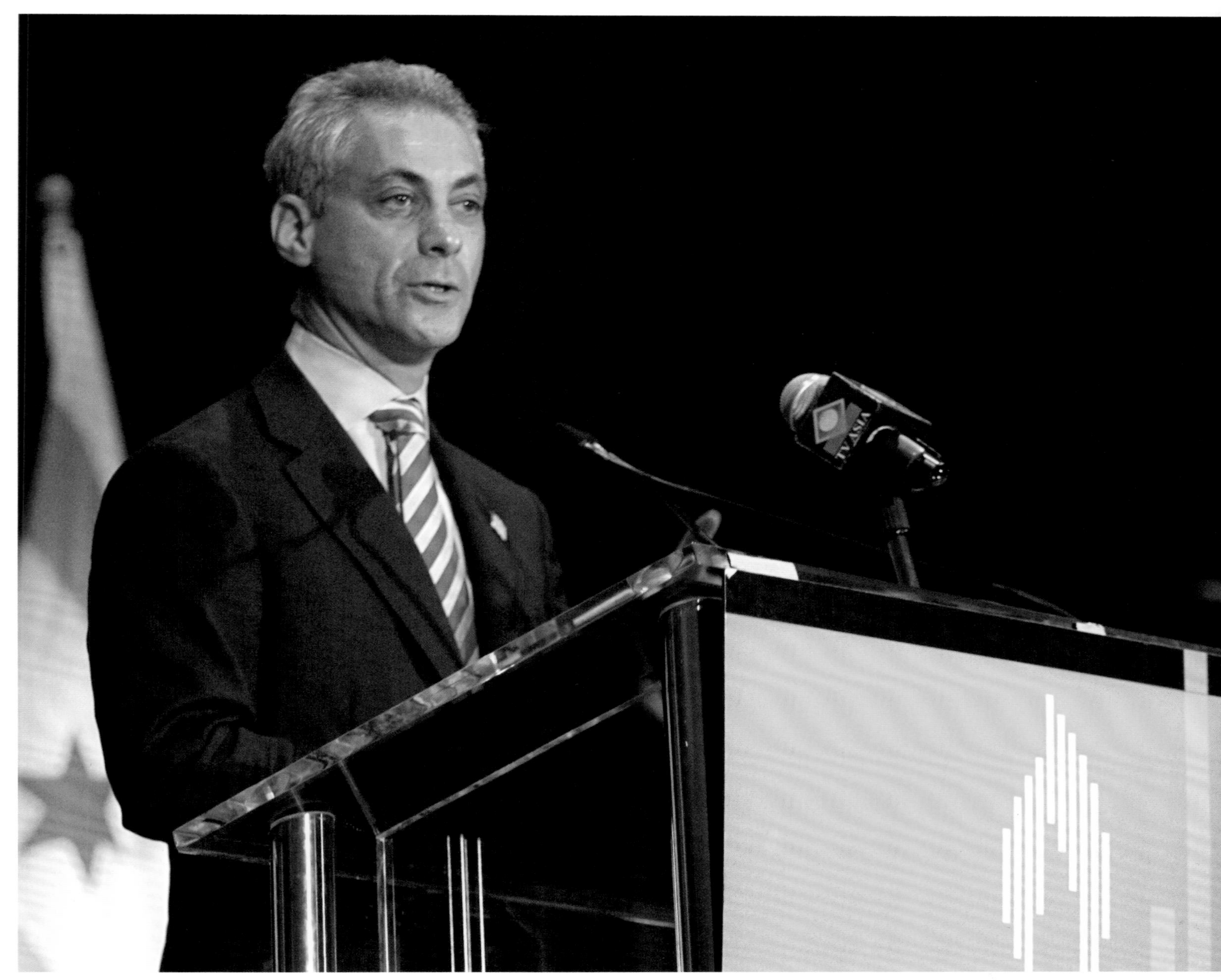

Shortly after being elected Chicago's 46th mayor, Mayor Rahm Emanuel made a commitment to support the mission of The Executives' Club of Chicago and actively collaborate with its members to advance the city's standing as a vibrant global business center.

The Executives' Club of Chicago has for a century served as a gathering place of ideas and inspiration to the thinkers and doers of this resilient city.

CHAPTER ONE

DEDICATED TO THE LIFE OF CHICAGO BUSINESS

A biting January wind hums with the busy midday traffic on South Michigan Avenue as men and women dressed for business flow through the front entrance of The Hilton Chicago. In the warmth of the historic hotel's open and opulent foyer they are guided up that familiar staircase framed by ornate marble columns and a second floor ceiling adorned with hand-painted frescoes. It's in the Versailles-inspired Grand Ballroom where the growing group comes together.

Despite the majesty of the room, the clatter of lively conversation mixed with the aroma of fresh coffee stirs an atmosphere resembling the excited anticipation of opening day at the ballpark. The mingling crowd at this casually refined reception, however, is gearing up for the calculated forecasts and persuasive points to be delivered at a luncheon that year-after-year examines the prospects of the local, national, and global economy. For The Executives' Club of Chicago, this is opening day.

The annual Economic Outlook Luncheon has long served as the opening event of this prestigious business organization each year, but never before have this many guests gathered for this colorfully candid prognosis of commerce and its implications from Wall Street to Main Street. The more than 1,700 men and women who gradually make their way from the Grand reception to their handsomely set tables in the hotel's International Ballroom surely recognize the particular significance of the program that is about to get underway. As the meeting is formally brought to order, they represent the innovative spirit and enduring success of a business forum celebrating its 100th anniversary.

On the stage at the head of the room, Craig S. Donohue, Chief Executive Officer of the CME Group and Chairman of the Board of The Executives' Club of Chicago in this milestone season, takes to the podium. He welcomes The Club's guests, members, and leaders to the first Centennial Signature Program and the kick-off to a year that will be commemorated with a dynamic slate of exceptional speakers, events, and programming. "This year is as much about our momentum going forward as it is a celebration of our rich history," says Donohue, before briefly outlining a strategic vision that builds on the organization's commitment to thought leadership, professional development, and best business practices.

Behind him, lean black banners that hang as a backdrop proclaim "Centennial

Craig S. Donohue, Chief Executive Officer of the CME Group and Chairman of the Board of The Executives' Club of Chicago in the first half of its Centennial Celebration, views this milestone as a guide to the future.

The Chicago Mercantile Exchange (CME) was among the organizations that in the early 1900s ushered in the open outcry era of public trading. Today more than 80 percent of its trades are processed electronically.

CME GROUP

When trading posts of early America opened along the Hudson River and Lake Michigan, New York and Chicago were destined to emerge as hubs of global commerce. As they did, trading became less isolated and more orchestrated. By the late 1800s, organizations like the Chicago Board of Trade (CBOT), the Chicago Butter and Egg Board, and the New York Merchants' Exchange (NYMEX) had been formed to regulate trade and manage risk through public trading methods called open outcry. In 1919, the Chicago Butter and Egg Board became the Chicago Mercantile Exchange (CME).

Beginning with leadership in agricultural commodities, CME's many milestones as a pioneer of the trading industry include its leap into financial futures with the launch of foreign exchange products in 1972. In embracing the advancing technology of the following decades, CME led the development of after-hours electronic trading systems for complex financial futures instruments. While maintaining the open outcry method of early public trading, the company introduced its CME Globex electronic trading platform in 1992, and today more than 80 percent of its trades are handled electronically.

The early incarnations of CME, CBOT, NYMEX, and COMEX linked buyers and sellers across land and sea. Today, these venerable organizations are formally unified under the corporate structure of CME Group. With CME's historic merger with CBOT in 2007 and acquisition of NYMEX in 2008, the company became CME Group, emerging as the world's leading derivatives marketplace. The combined organization continues to power the engine of global trade, offering the widest range of benchmark products across all major asset classes—including futures and options based on interest rates, equity indexes, foreign exchange, energy, agricultural commodities, metals, weather, and real estate.

Through its CME Globex electronic trading platform and its physical trading floor facilities in Chicago and New York, CME Group now operates 24 hours a day, seven days a week, in more than 85 countries around the world. In 2010, CME Group handled 3.1 billion contracts worth nearly $1 quadrillion in notional value.

CME laid the groundwork for its historic marriage with CBOT and NYMEX when it demutualized in 2000 and went public in 2002. Craig S. Donohue, Chief Executive Officer of CME Group, was instrumental in designing and achieving the demutualization and initial public offering, which made CME the first publicly traded financial exchange in the United States. "Like many exchanges, we had been organized as a membership or mutual organization for many decades, and as we confronted both technological change as well as the changing fabric of financial markets, it was very helpful for us to demutualize the company," said Donohue. "It allowed us to create a shareholder owned company focused on creating shareholder value. With that unifying principle, we were able to take a number of important steps forward."

Donohue has held a broad array of positions in his more than 20-year career with the company, including General Counsel and Chief Administrative Officer. He now leads a global workforce of more than 2,500 professionals working in specialized roles that range from financial technology development and risk management services to sales and marketing. "With a non-hierarchical type of structure, we encourage people to bring their ideas forward and foster debate as a way of reaching the right decisions," said Donohue. "While we might not be the fastest group to make a decision, generally speaking our decisions are well thought out with the point of view of, 'Will this

decision transcend time?' I think that's a key hallmark of this organization and one of the reasons we've been so successful."

Through its offices in New York, London, Singapore, Calgary, Houston, São Paulo, Seoul, Tokyo and Washington, D.C. as well as its Chicago headquarters, that success continues to add to local economies around the world. In Chicago alone, the company has a multi-billion dollar impact through revenues generated by the exchanges themselves and by traders, proprietary trading firms, software vendors, and clearing member firms. Every day, twice a day, CME Group moves between $6 billion and $10 billion of funds to and from market participants, with much of that banking activity occurring in Chicago.

With its trading infrastructure requiring fiber optic networks, high-speed lines, and energy and power redundancy, the company relies on its own expert team to develop the next generation of technologists through partnerships with Chicago area universities. To a great extent, technological innovation has enabled Chicago to reaffirm its leading role in the financial services industry.

"There's no doubt that Chicago has a tremendous pool of human capital and intellectual capital and it is a place where we've been able to harness the traditional Midwestern work ethic and values that really makes for successful business decision making," said Donohue. "At the same time, there's also a tremendous amount of creativity here, certainly in the financial market sense. After all, this is really where derivatives were invented and were cultivated to become a global phenomenon."

The focused creativity and phenomenal growth of CME and CME Group helped propel Chicago's rise as a global business center, and the company continues to cultivate its century-long relationship with the city. Through the CME Group Foundation, CME Group Community Foundation, CBOT Foundation and the company's community outreach program, CME Group's many philanthropic initiatives are designed to enhance economic opportunity and health and education, especially for disadvantaged youth in the communities where it does business.

Recognized in 2009 as The International Executive of the Year by The Executives' Club of Chicago and the Ernst & Young Entrepreneur of The Year® in the investment and financial services category for the Midwest region, Donohue views progress with a global perspective. Preparing a diverse workforce to meet the opportunities of change is just one of the elements that drives CME Group's vision of ongoing global growth, innovative product development, enhanced technology, and providing the highest level of service available on any exchange. "It's been a very important part of our heritage to really think about the future and the way our markets will be organized," said Donohue. "That perspective continues to help us determine what we need to do and the people we need to attract to stay competitive on the global stage."

NORTHERN TRUST

In August 1889, Byron Laflin Smith, one of the most respected bankers in Chicago at the time, established The Northern Trust Company to serve the city's affluent individuals and businesses. During the next decade, Northern Trust grew from a single room into a flourishing organization. Today it has become a global leader in delivering innovative investment management, asset and fund administration, and fiduciary and banking solutions to corporations, institutions and affluent individuals.

With a founding principle of adapting to the changing needs of its clients as well as its employees, Northern Trust created the very first life insurance trust in 1891 and introduced the first employee life insurance plan of its kind in 1912. In the 1950s, Northern Trust adapted to new advances in technology by automating banking processes and introducing new products. In 1962, it became one of the first financial institutions in the nation to process checks electronically. It was also in the 1960s that its clients began to develop business interests outside the United States, which led Northern Trust to open a London office in 1969. It was the first Illinois-chartered financial institution to open a branch outside the United States.

As global markets have become more fast-paced and complex in recent decades, Northern Trust has continued to establish new offices and develop new products and services to meet its clients' needs. Today, it is the largest administrator of offshore private equity funds in Europe, and one of the world's leading providers of institutional index management services. Northern Trust has also continued to advance a culture of community caring and support that has been central to its character since its humble beginnings.

Celebration 2011" in thin gold lettering. Underneath reads a boldly relevant tagline resurrected from a motto devised by the organization's leaders of long ago: "Global thinkers and doers since 1911." The banners also introduce a gold Centennial logo with an upward motion to signify the bar graphs that chart business growth and the brilliant vertical skyline that distinguishes the City of Chicago.

The extent to which this organization has contributed to the rise of such a flourishing modern landscape is impossible to measure, but over the last century The Executives' Club of Chicago has served as a central gathering place of ideas and inspiration to many of the brilliant thinkers and doers that have left their imprint on the city. Born before the First World War by a group of Chicago businessmen who began meeting to discuss business, make contacts and share experiences, the life of The Club parallels the progress of a city that established an early industrial foundation and steadily evolved into a world-class global business center.

As Chicago continues its march forward, so too does The Executives' Club of Chicago. Today, its more than 1,700 members are drawn to programming that offers them opportunities to meet with visionary business, government and academic leaders from around the world, become actively involved with colleagues and the larger business community, and gain insight into how their organizations can better compete in today's global economy.

In wrapping up his introductory remarks at the Economic Outlook Luncheon, Donohue offers gratitude to the corporations and organizations serving as Centennial Season Partners. He also acknowledges the many college students seated in the room.

The Club has for decades invited the students of local colleges and universities to its events. On this day, with the imagery of the Centennial banners that stand behind him, Donohue's recognition of these aspiring business leaders symbolizes the support The Club has provided to each generation before...and the promise of its service for generations to come.

A TRADITION OF SHARED PERSPECTIVES

Terry Savage is on the move. At the reception of the Economic Outlook Luncheon she glides from one group of familiar faces to the next. The enthusiasm of her exchanges isn't any surprise to those who have come to know her personally or peripherally through her nationally syndicated financial columns for the *Chicago Sun-Times,* her inimitable books on personal finance, and her frequent appearances as a speaker and television commentator. But with this Centennial Season opener also marking her 30th year as moderator of the Economic Outlook Luncheon, it seems there's an added sparkle to her smile.

The truth is, she has always viewed this forecasting forum as a celebration. Since beginning as a participant in 1980, Savage has recognized it as an opportunity for business leaders to come together to prime the engine of a new year—even, and perhaps especially, when the economy isn't encouraging a wave of optimism.

"This is my favorite event of the year," Savage says before making her way to the stage. "It's living proof that economics and economic forecasting doesn't have to be some dull thing with statistics and numbers."

While The Executives' Club has long cultivated presentations and conversations about economic health and opportunities, there was no formalized event evaluating the economy until 1980. At that time, it was called the Economic Forecast Luncheon, and Savage was the pioneering financial analyst of NBC's local news programming. She had already broken new ground as a founding member and the first woman trader on the Chicago Board Options Exchange. When she was asked to participate as a speaker, it was just as much a breakthrough for The Club.

"The meeting was held in the old Bismark Hotel, and there were probably only 10 women in the room," Savage recalls. "I made the bold prediction that interest rates, then at

Terry Savage was asked to lead the annual Economic Outlook Luncheon after participating in the inaugural event in 1980.

As a longtime leader who has helped organize other programs of The Club, Terry Savage sees inclusiveness as a primary key to its success.

about seven percent, would climb to over 10 percent. Everyone gasped." She made a friendly bet with one of her counterparts on the panel that day, and was proven prophetic when rates climbed to over 10 percent later in the year.

Savage's professional knack for delivering insight with exuberance made her a natural pick to lead the affair as its economic emcee. While her ability to bring out the best in the experts invited to opine each year has helped propel its success, she's quick to direct the credit to the panelists. "These are forecasters with tremendous personality and great track records," says Savage, who had also been a longtime Board member of The Club. "They jump right in there and disagree or agree strongly, and the audience loves it."

The Economic Outlook Luncheon is just one of the programs Savage has infused with energy over the years. In the early stages of her involvement with The Club, she saw the way its events drew the business community together. She can testify that forged relationships have led to productive partnerships, and that knowledge gained has been brought back to the office.

"Take a look at the crowds that attend our meetings now," she said after a luncheon in 2010. "They represent all stages of business success, from young people to entrepreneurs, corporate executives to financial services professionals, sales employees to advertising and marketing staff. It's important to them. It's important to the city. It's important to Chicago's reputation in the rest of the world that we have these great events put on by The Executives' Club. These events are interesting to everyone. They are not exclusive. They are inclusive and people attend not only to learn more, but also to meet more people."

On this day, most of the audience has already met the personalities that join Savage on stage. Dr. Bob Froehlich, Executive Vice President and Chief Investment Strategist for Wealth Management at The Hartford, and Jim Rogers, the noted author and successful international investor and adventurer, have each expressed their fiscal viewpoints at this event in years past. And, of course, there is Diane Swonk.

Like Savage, Swonk has become a mainstay of the Economic Outlook Luncheon. As a former Co-Chair of The Club's Finance Committee, she has been one of its lead organizers each year. Now the Chief Economist and Senior Managing Director at Mesirow Financial Holdings, Inc. and one of the most quoted economists in print, radio and television, Swonk recalls attending her first Economic Outlook Luncheon in the mid-1990s and thinking this is something she'd like to be a part of. "The very next year I was asked to participate," she says. "The forum is lively but it is also important because we're able to have a frank discussion about where the economy is heading and how it could impact the people in the room and the companies they represent."

Before Swonk and her fellow panelists address the room, the conversation at one table draws a consensus that business is looking better than the previous six months. The underscore to the dialogue centers on the recent announcement of tax hikes in Illinois and how

THE EXECUTIVES' CLUB
OF CHICAGO
CENTENNIAL CELEBRATION 2011
GLOBAL THINKERS AND DOERS SINCE 1911

International investor Jim Rogers can always be relied upon to offer colorfully candid views when he serves as a panelist at the annual Economic Outlook Luncheon.

companies based in the state will be able to continue to recover from the impact of the 2008 market collapse.

In her opening words, Savage acknowledges as much and cautions the crowd to consider the lessons of the past while building on the upsides of recent economic progress. At the 1981 event, when the national conversation also revolved around an unsure economy, she engaged the audience with questions that included: "How many people here think that we will enter a fairly steep recession this year? How many people think we will get through the year without too severe a recession? How about interest rates? How many people think that in the next eight weeks you will see a big decline in interest rates?" She has continued to bring the audience into the conversation, and this year is no different.

In their addresses, Froehlich and Swonk express confidence in the growing global economy but both are concerned about the state's choice to meet its fiscal deficit through increased taxes. "They are going to hit very hard and we need to have a real debate on what happens on the costs side," says Swonk. Rogers sees an economic upswing in the year ahead but views it as a momentary blip in a national crisis that isn't being properly addressed.

In the question and answer session that Savage leads at the end of the luncheon, the panelists expand on their assertions and trade both sobering and lighthearted moments that keep the record-breaking crowd in their seats until the meeting's official close. As those who have gathered for the opening event of the Centennial Season make their way out of The Hilton Chicago, they walk into the brisk air of a city that has carried on its business in all kinds of weather and no matter the challenges in its path.

INSPIRED BY THE MOMENTUM OF THE PAST

Since the early 19th century, economic cycles and business pursuits have been the building blocks of a city founded for its strategic trading value at the mouth of the Chicago River. Certainly, its ascendance as a center of commerce has been buoyed by its shoreline stance in the country's midsection, but each strand of Chicago's historical growth has been driven by the innovation and determination of its people.

Before Chicago was incorporated as a city in 1837, the corner of what is now Michigan

Dr. Bob Froehlich, Diane Swonk, and Jim Rogers each acknowledged the historic nature of the country's economic challenges, but had distinct perspectives on how long those challenges would continue.

Avenue and Wacker Drive was the site of the U.S. Army base known as Fort Dearborn. But in the years leading up to an attack by Native Americans in 1812 that saw it burn to the ground, and after the government rebuilt it in 1816, the area surrounding the fort was home to businessmen involved in the early fur trade. Now most familiar for the streets that bear their names, men that included John Kinzie, Gurdon Hubbard, and John Clark saw in the landscape off the shores of Lake Michigan its potential to be a vital asset to a country exercising a westward expansion.

William B. Ogden, who served as Chicago's first mayor, and other inspired leaders worked to mold an environment in which the city could begin to fulfill its promise. He was an instrumental supporter of the Illinois and Michigan Canal, a waterway completed in 1848 that linked the Great Lakes and the Mississippi River. This allowed the city's growing meatpacking industry and other young businesses to begin exporting goods to new markets. The railroads that soon followed, which Ogden also helped orchestrate, expanded the city's reach with their ability to carry passengers as well as commodities. Ogden and other business leaders then formed the Chicago Board of Trade in 1848 to support the physical avenues of trade and create a system in which crops harvested by farmers far from the city could be purchased in advance of their delivery in the warmer months.

By 1911, when a group of Chicago businessmen began meeting each week to discuss business issues and opportunities and build

BAXTER

Since the company's founding in 1931 as the first manufacturer of commercially prepared intravenous (IV) solutions, Baxter has become a leader in healthcare innovation worldwide. Other Baxter "firsts" include the first commercial kidney dialysis machine, the first concentrated clotting factor to treat hemophilia, and many other breakthroughs. More recently, the company was responsible for the first protein-free recombinant hemophilia therapy, and the first cell culture-based pandemic influenza vaccine.

Today, Baxter International Inc., through its subsidiaries, continues to develop, manufacture and market products that save and sustain the lives of people with hemophilia, immune disorders, infectious diseases, kidney disease, trauma, and other chronic and acute medical conditions. As a global, diversified healthcare company, Baxter applies a unique combination of expertise in medical devices, pharmaceuticals and biotechnology to create products that advance patient care worldwide.

Headquartered in Deerfield, Illinois, Baxter has nearly 48,000 employees globally. Its products are sold in more than 100 countries, with approximately 60 percent of the company's revenues coming from outside the United States.

In addition to its industry leadership, Baxter also is recognized as a leader in corporate sustainability. Baxter defines sustainability as the company's approach to including its social, economic and environmental responsibilities among its business priorities. Baxter gives back to the communities it serves through environmental stewardship, employee volunteerism, corporate giving and other initiatives. These efforts align with and support Baxter's mission to save and sustain lives.

Each meeting of The Executives' Club of Chicago, from ballroom engagements to intimate gatherings, is connected to the ideas and ambitions of The Club's earliest members.

business connections, pioneering department stores such as Marshall Field & Company and Carson Pirie Scott & Company had already emerged as retail leaders in the Midwest, and Montgomery Ward & Company and Sears, Roebuck & Company had established their niche in Chicago and beyond by following the idea that costs could be saved and customers could be reached through a mail order catalog strategy. Aaron Montgomery Ward actually worked for Marshall Field & Company for a time before launching, in 1872, what would become the world's first company of its kind. A decade later, Charles R. Walgreen, Sr., arrived in Chicago from downstate Dixon and began a series of jobs that would prepare him to open his own drugstore on the South Side in 1901.

And, of course, by the time the businessmen of The Executives' Club of Chicago held their first weekly meetings at the Hotel Sherman, the city's recovery from the Great Chicago Fire of 1871 was the stuff of legend. In fact, the original Hotel Sherman on the north side of Randolph Street between Clark and LaSalle was among the more than 18,000 structures leveled in the fire. It was part of the city's quite extraordinary and rapid rebuilding effort. That the response to the fire focused not only on rebuilding but improving and expanding the face of the city reflects the same innovation and collective determination of those who had spurred Chicago's growth at its very beginnings.

The second city that arose from the ashes of 1871—and celebrated its comeback as the host of the World's Columbian Exposition of 1893—was just as renowned for its architectural beauty as its entrepreneurial spirit and industrial edge. After all, the 45 men who made up the initial membership of The Executives' Club in 1911 were witness to the dedication in that year of the classical revival style City Hall that still stands on a full block in what is now the Loop. With the city's challenges and successes connecting one generation of citizens to the next, it's likely the founding fathers of The Executives' Club, like other Chicagoans of the day, saw themselves as responsible descendents of a resilient line of creative thinkers and doers.

ComEd, which would become one of Exelon's signature companies, was already an industry leader by 1920, when it counted 500,000 customers and nearly $40 million in annual revenues.

EXELON

In 1882, less than three years after Thomas Edison developed a practical light bulb, the Western Electric Company was founded in Chicago. In 1887, Western Electric became Chicago Edison, and in 1907 the company took the now-familiar name Commonwealth Edison, or ComEd. By 1920, ComEd counted 500,000 customers, 6,000 employees and nearly $40 million in annual revenues. By the 1990s, it had grown to 3.4 million customers and annual revenues of some $7 billion.

In 2000, ComEd merged with Philadelphia's PECO Energy Company. The new parent company took the name Exelon with headquarters in Chicago and approximately 12,000 employees in northern Illinois. Today, the Exelon family of companies includes Exelon Generation, ComEd, PECO and Exelon Transmission Company.

Just as Commonwealth Edison played an important role in America's economic progress. Exelon stands out as a leader of energy policy and development in the early 21st century. John W. Rowe, Chairman and Chief Executive Officer of Exelon, has attained international regard for his commitment to clean energy and competitive markets. His Exelon 2020 plan is a renowned business and environmental strategy for cleaning up the electricity supply in the most economic ways.

"Exelon 2020 is an industry-leading plan designed to reduce our environmental footprint at the lowest possible cost," Rowe said. "Through a focused range of initiatives such as exploring the opportunities of natural gas and other energy sources, increasing the output of our nuclear plants, and instituting customer conservation programs, the goal of this strategic vision is to shrink our carbon footprint by more than 15 million metric tons of greenhouse gas emissions per year by 2020." Exelon is halfway to its goal, having eliminated the equivalent annual emissions of approximately 1.5 million cars.

While working toward a clean energy future, Exelon and its subsidiaries—Exelon Generation, ComEd and PECO—have earned a reputation as companies at the forefront of corporate responsibility. Each has a long-standing tradition of supporting and strengthening the communities it serves. For example, in 2010 alone, Exelon distributed nearly $18 million in grants to nonprofit organizations, and more than 2,000 Exelon employees recorded nearly 66,000 hours of volunteer community service. Exelon's senior management team and other employees serve on the boards of more than 350 nonprofit organizations throughout the Chicago and Philadelphia areas. These efforts earned it the designation of Corporate Volunteer Program of the Year in 2008, 2009 and 2010 from VolunteerMatch, a national nonprofit focused on engaging volunteers.

In 2010, the Chicago History Museum presented its Cyrus H. McCormick History Maker Award for Historic Corporate Achievement to Exelon for its sustained and ardent support of the community.

"Whether it's Chicago or Philadelphia, the emphasis within Exelon on being a productive part of the cities in which we work is not unique to any of our CEOs past or present," Rowe said. "It is a commitment that has been part of our company's culture throughout its history, and it goes hand-in-hand with our business priority of becoming a cleaner and greener company that continues to provide exemplary service that meets the energy needs of our customers."

1911–1940

BUILDING ON AN AMBITIOUS FOUNDATION

Distinguished by its sandy brick façade and the elegant white mantle of its tops floors, The Hotel Sherman stood on the site that now holds the Thompson Center. Throughout the 1910s and roaring '20s, the hotel was one of Chicago's premier nightspots. While the live jazz presented in its College Inn restaurant attracted celebrities, tourists, and members of high society in the evenings, it was during the day that members of The Executives' Club met each Friday in the hotel's Louis XIV Room.

In its first several years, the core of The Club discussed among themselves the affairs of the day and the business impact. In sharing their experiences as well, they looked for ways to learn from one another and work with each other on the business front. They perhaps talked of new ventures that could benefit from the success of Chicago's retail companies or examined the strategies that enabled Samuel Insull, through his leadership of Commonwealth Edison, to expand the company's hold on electric power in the Midwest.

Like many other Chicagoans, their attention in 1914 surely turned to the local affects of the U.S. decision to enter the First World War in support of Great Britain, France, and Russia. With many of the area's young men sent overseas after their training at Fort Sheridan and the Great Lakes Naval Training Center north of the city, employment opportunities emerged for women and African Americans. The Great Migration of African Americans from the South to industrial cities like Chicago continued after the war came to a close in 1918.

When the economy sparked in the 1920s, The Executives' Club sought new members. Membership was open to men "holding an executive position, either as an owner, partner, department manager, or official of the company he represents," according to The Club's material of the time. Dues were $16 a year, payable in advance.

To meet the needs of its growing flock The Club began to feature speakers at its weekly meetings. Typically, the presentations related to the business practices of members. On Friday, November 20, 1925, its luncheon program featured William K. Braasch, President of The Salesmanship Foundation. In advance of Braasch's keynote, titled "The Conquest of Fear," The Club's newsletter promoted the event with a profile that concluded: "...It is the conviction of your Speakers Committee that no member of this club can hear this message—vital to business men generally—and leave the meeting without having secured many definite and concrete pointers which can be advantageously used in his own business."

Yet, The Club's lineup of notable business speakers was soon balanced by presentations that ventured into more cultural, philosophical and even geological territory. In April of 1926, the famous Arctic explorer Commander Donald B. MacMillan engaged the Friday luncheon crowd with his adventurous

"Flying for Fun"

By AMELIA EARHART
World's Premiere Aviatrix

Miss Earhart might very properly be called, "America'
heart" and it is indeed, a real pleasure to announce
speaker this week. She will tell us her story of aviation

Miss Earhart is an accomplished speaker. Her ch
is as notable as the grace and modesty which have
tionate admiration of the world. In her lectures,
the Atlantic flight, but also tells of her other
meaning and possibilities of flying in general, e
women. The story she tells holds a wealth o
toned with whimsical humor.

This will be one of the banner meetings
unusually large attendance to greet our dis
a cordial invitation to the ladies to grace this au

NOTE: We broadcast at 1:00 p. m. over KYW
Tell your friends to tune in

AND!
MISS BETTY ALLEN
Leading Lady of "Take a Chance"
now playing at Erlanger Theatre
MISS LEIGHTON EDELEN, Accompanist

OUR NEXT MEETING
October 27th
WHITING WILLIAMS
"Stalin, Mussolini or Roosevelt—
Which Has the Answer?"

ANNIVERSARY PARTY
April 17, 1936
6:30 P. M. FRIDAY, APRIL 17th
HOTEL SHERMAN—Grand Ball Room
Dinner—Entertainment
Dancing—Bridge
Al Trace & His Orchestra
INFORMAL
Bring wife, sweetheart, guests—or come alone.

There will be Surprises and Prizes and more Surprises

ADDED FEATURE!
Abe Lyman
IN PERSON
WILL PRESENT FOR YOUR APPROVAL ACTS FROM HIS
NEW COLLEGE INN FLOOR SHOW

THE BIGGEST AND BEST CELEBRATION
IN THE HISTORY OF THE EXECUTIVES' CLUB
Send in your RESERVATION AT ONCE to the Club Office
HURRY! HURRY!

Next Meeting April 24, 1936. Rufus R. Dawes, President Museum of Science and Industry.
Talk and Pictures.

Address Broadcast at 1 P. M. by Station WMAQ

AND!
DU PAGE COUNTY AMERICAN LEGION
DRUM AND BUGLE CORPS

explorations far from Chicago in a talk titled, "The Arctic by Sea, Land, and Air." A month later, on May 7, 1926, Arthur Perrow of the Illinois Bell Telephone Company discussed methods of managing an efficient workforce.

Authors, educators, actors and bankers were all part of the mix. While membership was not yet open to women, it was also in 1926 that The Club began issuing invitations to women for special "Ladies' Day" programs—though many of these uplifting events were held in the evening. One Wednesday evening in November of 1928 featured a popular poet psychologist on "The Exact Science of Cracking Jokes."

The Club adopted a logo that depicted "The Thinker," by French sculptor Auguste Rodin, accompanied by the motto, "The thinker...and doer," which like today, expressed The Club's desire to promote dialogue that leads to action. The Club also made clear its priority of supporting education. The Club's leaders at the time described the organization as "a continuing school that keeps its members up-to-date, not only in business and financial affairs, but in the culture side of life."

By this time, The Club was encouraging its members to bring a friend. Though many of its programs aired on local radio, prospective members were more likely to join after experiencing its speakers firsthand. Reflecting the rhythm of the era and the reputation of the Hotel Sherman, these meetings were often accented with live musical entertainment. The Club made frequent use of the hotel's Grand Ballroom as its events began to draw more than 500 members and guests. For those who missed a meeting, the presentations of many of its speakers were published in full in The Club's weekly newsletter. It was also through The Executives' Club News that members and others learned about The Club's social events, which included golf outings, theater visits, and holiday parties.

While social functions strengthened bonds among members and the more lighthearted speakers contributed to the social vibe of the city, the bulk of The Club's early thought leadership programs focused on domestic concerns as well as growing global issues.

In January of 1928, David R. Forgan, Vice-Chairman, National Bank of the Republic—Chicago, visited The Club to discuss "Our Foreign Debts." Unlike the dialogue of today, Forgan's focus was on the mechanisms America can and should use to, over time, collect reparations from the countries it supported and battled in World War I. Later in the year, Judge Frank Comerford offered insight on the workings of the Criminal Branch of the Superior Court.

Despite the pains of The Great Depression, The Club continued to thrive after 1929 and sought out speakers working at the frontlines of the national crisis. In 1933, Patrick Hurley, Secretary of War under President Herbert Hoover, spoke about the New Deal and the road to economic recovery. But it was also in this year that The Club landed a speaker who had become a national treasure.

When the airline industry was developing its plans to move from mail carrying to passenger travel—in 1927 William Boeing founded Boeing Air Transport Co., which would later spawn United Airlines in Chicago—Amelia Earhart was capturing the attention of the world with her pioneering triumphs in aviation. In 1928, as a passenger, she became the first woman to fly across the Atlantic Ocean. Later that year, as a solo pilot, she became the first woman to fly across North America.

A graduate of Hyde Park High School in Chicago, Earhart drew an overflow crowd of men and women to the Grand Ballroom of the Hotel Sherman when she addressed The Club on October 20, 1933. Reflecting on her ambitions and adventures, she acknowledged and identified with the women in the room. "Wherever I go I am mistaken for practically every other woman who gets her name in the papers now and then," she said. "Sometimes I am confused as to my own identity. I can't tell you how many times I have been congratulated for swimming the English Channel." She returned to The Club in October of 1935. Her mysterious disappearance while attempting to circumnavigate the globe came two years later.

After The Club celebrated its Silver Anniversary in 1936—a grand affair of dinner, dancing, and live music—it established a collection of organizational committees and continued to present an array of thought leaders that in the late 1930s ranged from the former president of the Illinois Bar Association and the governor of Minnesota to the president of DePaul University and a world famous magician. Women speakers became more frequent but three more decades would pass before they were admitted as members.

By 1940, with close to 1,000 men filling its membership and Chicago benefiting from the strides of local companies exploring research and technology—including Motorola, Baxter Laboratories, and Abbott Laboratories—The Club was poised to carry on as a forum that supported the city's efforts to overcome a still suffering national economy. Research based in Chicago would soon play a powerful role in the country's involvement in another World War, and The Executives' Club of Chicago would serve as a gathering place to discuss its implications.

The Executives' Club NEWS

Published Weekly by The Executives' Club

CHICAGO, U. S. A. JANUARY 20, 1928

VOL. 4

12:00 Noon, Friday, January 20th—Hotel Sherman

"OUR FOREIGN DEBTS"

By David R. Forgan

Vice-Chairman, National Bank of the Republic—Chicago

Every member of the Executives' Club will be interested in hearing an old friend of ours, Mr. David R. Forgan, one of Chicago's leading bankers, discuss the timely subject: "Our Foreign Debts."

Mr. Forgan for more than thirty years has occupied a very prominent position in the banking world of Chicago and of this country, having been in the positions of vice-president, president, and vice-chairman of four of Chicago's outstanding banks.

Who's Who in America states that he began his banking career at the age of fifteen. Surely this is exhibiting the Scotch trait namely: the study and the consideration of finance at an unusually early age, and he has been in continuous banking service ever since; though being a man of many talents, he has achieved distinction in writing, particularly along the line of finance.

However, he is known to his friends as a man of fine sentiment, a poet, and an artist.

As a speaker, he is remarkable for his clarity of thought, his ability to state in simple and interesting words complex and more or less distant ideas and conceptions of credits. On this subject he is an authority. He has a vein of Scotch humor that is frequently exhibited in laying up some intricate or involved phase of his subject. He never ... make an appeal to his audience.

... like him and you will come away with a clear and definite ... that constitutes our foreign debts.

... cannot remember the first time he borrowed from ... if it was a loan that he was in doubt of getting. He ... mingled feeling of doubt, triumph, and the satisfac... carrying away the money, and later the triumphant ... ion within himself when he paid the loan back on time ... himself as a man whose word was good at the bank.

... has an advantage in discussing this subject, because he ... otland, and therefore knows the foreign financial situa... oughly and the feeling of our foreign creditors.

...arly and bring a friend as we are going to have a large audience for this rema...

Address Broadcast at 1:00 p. m. by Station WMAQ

W. C. DORNFIELD

Late Star of the Elsie Janis Sho...

In Tricks and Chatter

Courtesy of Benso...

The Executives' Club NEWS

VOL. 2

Published Weekly by The Executives' Club

CHICAGO, U. S. A. APRIL 9, 1926

No. 27

RED LETTER DAY—NOTE CHANGE OF TIME

12 Noon, Sharp, Friday, April 9—Hotel Sherman

"THE ARCTIC By SEA, LAND and AIR"

With Motion Pictures

By Commander Donald B. Mac Millan

FAMOUS ARCTIC EXPLORER

Our Aim—Biggest Day we ever had—1000 Members and Guests present

DONALD B. Mac MILLAN one of the most indomitable of all those adventurous men who "leaves safety first" behind in his aim to bring back, from unknown fields, facts for use in all branches of Science. He will tell us a graphic story.

Mr. MacMillan is now preparing to leave for his 10th trip.

Maria Wynne, CEO, Girl Scouts of Greater Chicago & Northwest Indiana, was among many esteemed guests who shared stories, explored issues, and offered advice at The Club's Women's Leadership Centennial Summit.

CHAPTER TWO

DISTINGUISHED BY INDIVIDUALS AND IDEAS

With her appearance at the Women's Leadership Centennial Summit serving as a homecoming of sorts—and her having since gained another "first" as a female leader—Christine Lagarde's luncheon address was certainly one to remember.

The head table stretched across the front of the room and blanketed in white is empty, except for the podium and microphone that stand at its center. Every other table in the International Ballroom at the Hilton Chicago, however, is becoming filled with guests who are eager to take in the words and wisdom of one of the most recognized and admired women in the world.

The voice of Mary MacLaren, Executive Director of The Club, cuts through the buzz of pre-lunch conversation as she begins to introduce the distinguished occupants of this program's head table. The room grows quiet.

Anyone who has attended a formal event of The Executives' Club in recent years is familiar with its tradition of inviting local and visiting business leaders as well as particular Board members, committee leaders, and special guests to join the featured speaker of the day on the dais. Part of this tradition, as MacLaren reminds the room, is that the assembled hold their applause for these leaders until all have been introduced. On this day, in late March of 2011, that tradition is broken not once but twice.

As MacLaren announces "Her Excellency Christine Lagarde," the statuesque Minister for Economy, Finance and Industry of the Republic France appears at the right of the elevated stage. She makes her way toward the center of the head table and, beaming a wide smile at the crowd, she is greeted back with reserved applause that builds momentum until MacLaren continues with the introductions.

The emanating warmth of this break with tradition has as much to do with Lagarde's triumphant return to a city she refers to as her second home as it does her global prominence as the first female finance minister of a leading industrialized country. She is here at The Executives' Club's full-day Women's Leadership Centennial Summit to keynote its Global Woman Leader of the Year Luncheon and accept the organization's first Global Woman Leader of the Year Award.

It was in Chicago that the affable and out-spoken Lagarde raised her leadership profile as Chairman of the Chicago-based global law firm Baker & McKenzie. In her six years at the firm and in the city, beginning in 1999, she served as a member of the Board and Secretary of the Board of The Executives' Club. At this homecoming of sorts, Lagarde epitomizes the summit's overarching title, "Women of Consequence: Building Financial, Political and Corporate Clout."

Yet, as MacLaren nears the end of her introduction of the head table, she announces the name of another woman of consequence that Chicago has long admired, one whose presence on this day seems to catch the audience by surprise. There is a short pause after MacLaren declares, "First Lady of Chicago Maggie Daley."

Mrs. Daley, on the rebound from illnesses both related and unrelated to the metastatic cancer she was diagnosed with in 2002, steps onto the dais and the crowd rises to its feet in rousing applause. With her husband in the midst of wrapping up his six-term, 22-year run as Chicago's mayor, this ovation clearly conveys genuine appreciation for her dignity and grace as Chicago's first lady and her passionate support of children, education, the arts, and the unified strength of Chicago's business community.

Daley and Lagarde, who became close during Lagarde's years in Chicago, meet and embrace at the center of the head table. Together, they exemplify the impact of those who were born in Chicago, those who have come here to pursue worthy ambitions, and those who have extended the city's reach and influence. On this day, at the Women's Leadership Centennial Summit, they also symbolize the vitality of women and celebrate The Executives' Club of Chicago's ongoing commitment to nurturing women as leaders in business, politics, and beyond.

THE CHARACTER TO CREATE LASTING IMPRESSIONS

A memorable moment it was. But for the women and the impressive showing of men who took part in the Women's Leadership

Centennial Summit, it was one of many that highlighted the March 25th affair.

Before this event arrived, The Club already had the momentum of hosting seven distinct programs in its Centennial Season, and it would soon honor another well-known Chicago business leader with its International Executive of the Year Award.

In January, The Club's Communications Committee Breakfast followed the Economic Outlook Luncheon by just five days. Led by Tonise Paul, President and CEO of Energy BBDO, the panel of savvy business personalities explored effective marketing strategies in a new age. The Women's Leadership Breakfast in January outlined tips on being a powerful negotiator.

The parade of programming continued in February and March. "Managing Up: How to Form an Effective Relationship with Those Above You" was the focus of the New Leaders Circle Leadership Development Program; Vikram Pandit, the CEO of Citigroup, explained the importance of financial inclusion at the Global Leaders Luncheon; and Staci Trackey Meagher, the General Manager,

Before Lagarde and Daley (opposite page) energized the audience at the Women of Consequence event, The Club had already established its centennial momentum with a Chicago CEO Breakfast with Mary Dillon (below left), the President and CEO of U.S. Cellular, and a Global Leaders Luncheon featuring Jeffrey Immelt (below right), the Chairman and CEO of General Electric.

Under the leadership of Tonise Paul, Energy BBDO has become a fully integrated communications organization that continues to build on its history of delivering powerfully creative solutions for clients.

ENERGY BBDO

In reflecting on her company's past, Tonise Paul is more likely to describe the images and inspiration of successful advertising campaigns than the elements of internal company structures. As President and Chief Executive Officer of Energy BBDO, the Chicago unit of Omnicom-owned BBDO Worldwide, Paul and the talented team she has assembled over the years have relied on that instinctual sense of storytelling to solidify Energy BBDO's place as a leading creative organization dedicated to energizing people and brands.

"We've had the pleasure and privilege of working with some great iconic brands, both in the U.S. and around the world," said Paul, who is also a Director of BBDO Worldwide, which is the second largest advertising agency network in the world. "The work we have produced to build our clients' brands and drive their business is what continues to drive our business as well."

Originally founded in 1932 as Arthur Meyerhoff Associates, the Chicago agency was acquired by BBDO Worldwide in 1979. It wasn't until 2005 that it took the name Energy BBDO to better represent its unique mission. BBDO itself was formed through a merger of Barton, Durstine & Osborn, and the Batten Company back in 1928. Since that time, the New York-based company has grown into a worldwide network that now operates 287 offices in 79 countries, and has been consistently named the most awarded agency network in the world for creativity and effectiveness.

Paul joined BBDO's Chicago office in 1983 as an Account Executive and went on to hold every account leadership position including EVP, Director of Client Services prior to becoming CEO in 1996. Since being reborn with a name that reflects its creative spirit and capabilities, Energy BBDO has continued to build an impressive client roster that today includes Bayer, Wm. Wrigley Jr. Company, Henkel, the Illinois Lottery, Art Institute of Chicago and the Chicago White Sox, among others.

The agency has a track record of recognition and industry accolades for effective and imaginative work for its diverse range of clients. Recent awards include honors from the Cannes Lions, Effies, the One Show, CLIOs, London International Awards, Communication Arts and others.

Under Paul's leadership, the agency has become a fully integrated communications organization and has experienced significant growth. "With a strong and growing marketing sciences practice and a thriving digital practice known as Proximity Chicago, we are very multifaceted," said Paul. "Clients want more from us than a 30-second television spot or a print ad. They're looking to us to deliver holistic, creative solutions to a variety business problems, and we can bring them together in a powerful overall creative solution that positively impacts their business."

At Energy BBDO, powerful creative solutions typically begin with extensive market research. For the launch of Wrigley's 5 gum, the agency focused on the insight that teens and young adults inherently crave the thrill of the unknown. By tapping into their deepest desires for experimentation, sensory stimulation and discovery, Energy BBDO and Wrigley were able to create a multi-layered consumer journey that successfully re-stimulated the category's heaviest chewers and led to the most successful gum launch in the company's history. For the Art Institute of Chicago (AIC), Energy BBDO brought the dynamic element of personal engagement to AIC's "500 Ways of Looking at Modern" campaign. To celebrate the opening of the museum's Modern Wing, 500 red

cubes—reminiscent of the AIC logo—were scattered around the City of Chicago, causing people to be surprised and intrigued in the same way they are during a visit to the Art Institute itself. When discovered, the cubes led people to visit 500-Ways.com, where they were assigned an art project that would be uploaded, admired and discussed on the website and showcased in a special exhibition in the Modern Wing. The campaign built an online community around the AIC by bringing art directly to Chicagoans, and reignited emotional investment in the institution.

With research inspiring creativity, Energy BBDO has cultivated a culture where optimism and openness are part of a collaborative process that extends to clients. "We know that the best thinking comes from the sparks that fly when we work together with each other and our client organizations," said Paul.

Viewing this collective pursuit as the key to its success as a creative services organization, the company continues to make a priority of attracting and retaining the most talented people in the industry. In fact, the *Chicago Tribune* named Energy BBDO one of Chicago's Top Workplaces for 2010. "You have to win the right people before you can win anything else, and we take great pride in being able to sustain and strengthen a team that is among the very best," said Paul.

In the last decade, strengthening its team and its services has revolved around integrating new technologies that have enhanced the agency's ability to serve clients in more than 40 countries. "We collaborate every day with partners across the world," said Paul. "In our dynamic industry, clients are seeking compelling insights and category-breaking creativity. We're able to use new and innovative tools to express our clients' brands to the consumer and to involve the consumer with our brands."

The agency's embrace of growth and progress while remaining true to its focus of producing work that energizes people and brands reflects the global stature and honest, hard-working ethic of Chicago. "I don't think it's any surprise that some of the biggest and best global companies are based here in Chicago," said Paul. "It is an epicenter of the world, and when you consider the technology and the talent that is available in this market because of the world-class academic institutions, I don't know a better place for a business to grow and thrive than in the City of Chicago."

With Chicago serving as an instrument of the agency's vision, Energy BBDO continues to build on its momentum as a bold leader in the creative industry. "The opportunity to come together to deliver creative ideas for brands around the world is an exciting and exhilarating experience that keeps us moving forward every day," said Paul. "The promise of our future is great because it is imbedded in the talent that we have attracted as an organization. And that talent is better than ever."

Midwest District, of Microsoft Corporation, moderated a fascinating tech talk with expert panelists at the season's first Technology Conference.

Weeks later, members and guests heard from two of today's most respected business leaders. At the Global Leaders Luncheon on March 8, Jeffrey Immelt, the Chairman and CEO of General Electric and the newly named Chairman of President Barack Obama's Council on Jobs and Competitiveness, offered a blueprint for global competitiveness. On March 17th, speaking at the Chicago CEO Breakfast, Mary Dillon, the President and CEO of U.S. Cellular, connected the dots of what consumers want, how companies are responding, and where the wireless industry is headed.

With Dillon's appearance setting the stage for the Women's Leadership Centennial Summit, the day dedicated to Women of Consequence got off to a smart start with a breakfast of salmon and eggs served with a wide-ranging discussion on "Securing Your Financial Future." Moderated by Terry Savage, the morning's panelists shared valuable lessons and practical financial guidance wrapped in personal stories.

Stephanie Neely, Chicago's treasurer, emphasized the importance of financial literacy. She grew up on the South Side after her family moved to Chicago from rural Mississippi. "As a 15-year-old kid I balanced the family checkbook," she said. Susan Whiting, Vice Chairman and Chief Diversity Officer of The Nielsen Company, talked about how making a long-term plan in your career and with your finances can bring balance and direction to a busy life. Ellen Rogin, President of Strategic Financial Designs, recounted the bold steps she took when she decided to return to the workforce after having children. On the financial side, she ultimately summarized by keeping it simple. "Don't spend more than you earn," she said.

Two other morning sessions drew in the Summit's guests before Lagarde was honored at the luncheon. Kapila Anand, National Partner-in-Charge, Public Policy Business Initiatives at KPMG, facilitated a conversation among a panel of leaders with deep board experience on the elements to consider before and after joining an organization's board. "Boards need the best people, not best friends," reminded Susan Schiffer Stautberg, Co-Founder and Co-Chair of WCD and President of PartnerCom Corporation. Guests of the Summit then shifted to a dialogue on the role of women in politics that included Toni Preckwinkle, President of the Cook County Board. She and the other panelists discussed the opportunities and obstacles of their public service and encouraged more women to add their voice to issues they care about.

Ironically, another woman with political accomplishments would add her voice to the sounds of the Summit at the end of the day's events. Melissa Bean, the former U.S. Representative from the 8th Congressional District of Illinois, had been recently named President and CEO of The Executives' Club of Chicago when she introduced herself to members and guests at The Women

Members of a Beijing troupe perform a Chinese Long Sleeve Dance at the gala for Baker & McKenzie's 2011 Annual Partners Meeting. The dance was developed in ancient China for royalty and nobles to celebrate grand occasions.

BAKER & MCKENZIE

Nine years after the 1911 founding of The Executives' Club of Chicago, a young man schooled in the ways of the American West road on a cattle train from his home in New Mexico to enroll in the University of Chicago. His name was Russell Baker. He was just 19, but he already personified The Club's slogan—"the thinker ... and doer."

Like The Executives' Club, Baker saw opportunity for thoughtful men (and women) of action in the great city he would come to call home and in the world beyond America's borders. At a time of isolationist sentiment following World War I, Baker embraced the internationalist views of his favorite professors. He began to formulate the forward-thinking ideas that eventually would give his name to the world's first global law firm.

It would be 29 years, a successful legal career, and another world war before he would join litigator John McKenzie in creating Baker & McKenzie. Not just another law firm, but one with a pioneering global vision. A firm without nationality or borders. A truly global firm that today is led by chairman Eduardo Leite, born in Uruguay and admitted in Brazil, and counts among its alumni Christine Lagarde, the Managing Director of the International Monetary Fund.

The DNA of the firm, which today has been recognized as the "strongest law firm brand in the world," was forged in offices in downtown Chicago, annual meetings around the world (including most recently in the Great Hall of the People in Beijing), and in the kiva carved out of a ravine behind the Baker home in Lake Bluff. Passionately global. A culture of friendship. Commercially pragmatic. Ahead of the curve.

Baker became a member of The Executives' Club of Chicago in 1951, two years after starting the firm that today has 3,800 locally admitted lawyers in 42 countries. It was the first major law firm with partners and offices on all six broadly inhabited continents—the first with $1 billion in fees and the first to elect a woman as its chairman, Ms. Lagarde.

Today, Baker & McKenzie provides legal services to more than half the world's largest corporations, including many headquartered in Chicago such as Abbott Laboratories (an original Russell Baker client), Kraft Foods, McDonald's, Motorola, and Boeing. The Firm's lawyers are citizens of more than 50 countries. They speak more than 75 languages. Global fees exceed $2.2 billion.

Some of the Firm's most rewarding work is done *pro bono*, in collaboration with clients. For example: Teaming with lawyers from Accenture, Caterpillar and Merck to advise PILnet, a public interest law institute, in developing model legislation to protect women from sexual exploitation in the workplace in Nepal; collaborating with counsel from Microsoft to help the International Federation of the Red Cross and Red Crescent Societies develop model legislation to enable swifter, more effective response to natural disasters; and working with lawyers from Starbucks on analysis of truth and reconciliation commissions for the Public International Law and Policy Group. The Executives' Club of Chicago. Baker & McKenzie. Thinkers and doers.

Each meeting of The Club is organized and executed by its determined staff in collaboration with a team of dedicated partners.

AON
22
39

Right: Deloitte's offices at 111 South Wacker Drive house more than 3,700 professionals who are committed to serving their clients and Chicago's communities with distinction.

Far right: Deloitte professionals gather to celebrate IMPACT Day, the organization's annual national volunteer day of service celebrating their year-round commitment to driving meaningful change in our local communities.

DELOITTE

In the professional services industry, Deloitte LLP is a name synonymous with quality, integrity, business acumen, and corporate responsibility. After all, the accounting practice started in London by William Welch Deloitte in 1845 has been serving clients longer than any organization in the independent auditing profession.

A pioneer in the profession, W.W. Deloitte eventually set his sights on America, opening an office in New York in 1880 and one in Chicago in 1912. American accountants and auditors made equally invaluable contributions to furthering the profession. Among them were Charles Waldo Haskins and Elijah Watt Sells whose firm Haskins & Sells undertook, in 1893, the first comprehensive revision of the federal government's accounting practices since George Washington. For his part, the Scotsman George Touche opened an office in New York in 1900 and by the 1960s his firm, Touche Ross, was a leader in the new field of management consulting. In 1968, Admiral Nobuzo Tohmatsu, a founding father of modern accounting in Japan, founded his own firm, Tohmatsu & Co.

In time, the firms of Deloitte, Haskins & Sells, Touche Ross, and Tohmatsu & Co. would help set new standards for the profession, both in the U.S. and around the world. A series of mergers and acquisitions in the final decades of the 20th century led by Edward A. Kangas of Touche Ross, J. Michael Cook of Deloitte Haskins & Sells, and Iwao Tomita of Tohmatsu & Co. transformed Deloitte into a global leader and innovator in professional services.

Today, approximately 182,000 dedicated professionals in Deloitte member firms in more than 150 countries collaborate to provide audit, tax, consulting and financial advisory services to public and private companies of all sizes in 20 industries. The firms are members of Deloitte Touche Tohmatsu Limited (DTTL), a UK private company.

Deloitte LLP, the U.S. member firm of DTTL, employs a workforce of more than 56,000 professionals, including more than 3,700 in Chicago, who help its clients address their most pressing and complex business issues. Deloitte has been the largest professional services organization in Chicago for many years and recently added the same accolade nationally.

"We're incredibly proud of this milestone," said Deborah L. DeHaas, vice chairman and Central region managing partner for Deloitte LLP. "It's a reflection of our shared set of core values rooted in collaboration, ethics, outstanding client service and commitment to diversity and leadership development."

DeHaas has spent her entire 30-year career in Chicago and has served in many leadership positions for Deloitte as well as in the city's business and civic communities. She has been a board member of The Executives' Club for the past 11 years and currently serves as second vice chair. As Central region managing partner for Deloitte, DeHaas leads the quality, client satisfaction, growth, marketplace and human resource initiatives for a 12-state region that encompasses 23 offices and nearly 9,000 professionals. She works closely with Stacy Janiak, managing partner of Deloitte's Chicago office, to drive marketplace growth and talent development locally. The Chicago office has grown into one of Deloitte's largest locations in the U.S. under their leadership.

Deloitte demonstrates its dedication to the Chicago marketplace by supporting many civic organizations such as The Executives' Club of Chicago. This important, long-standing relationship began in 2002 and includes support of the CEO Breakfast Series that provides local executives with a platform to share their insights and strategies for business success with their fellow leaders. Deloitte was also a proud supporter of The Club's Centennial season and worked with it on a number of innovative programs to celebrate its success.

Beyond its relationship with The Executives' Club, Deloitte's deep commitment to Chicago is evident in its multi-faceted community involvement strategy. Deloitte professionals volunteer in a variety of ways to assist nonprofit organizations by working on pro bono and skills-based projects and serving on boards of directors. The firm launched its robust pro bono program with a $50 million investment nationally over a three-year period. In Chicago, Deloitte's professionals have worked with organizations like the Chicago Public Schools, Chicago 2016, the United Way of Metropolitan Chicago, City Year Chicago and many others on pro bono projects that left a lasting legacy within the city's communities. Other initiatives, such as its annual IMPACT Day and Center for Community & Leadership seminars, allow Deloitte professionals to donate their time, skills and experiences to help nonprofits tackle business challenges. Deloitte is also recognized by the United Way as one of the top donors to its annual corporate giving campaign and as a leading pro bono organization.

Furthermore, Deloitte is focused on doing its part to develop a workforce that is equipped with the right skills to effectively compete in the global economy. The organization has concentrated its efforts on improving education, developing the skills of its people, increasing diversity, and understanding generational differences. In 2010, Deloitte created its national Future Fund to provide grants and assist organizations like City Year, United Way, Chicago Scholars, The Posse Foundation, After School Matters, and Ladder Up in their work to improve high school graduation rates and college enrollment among Chicago's students.

Additionally, the organization's enduring commitment to talent development took a bold step forward with the 2011 opening of Deloitte University. The new 107-acre facility located near Dallas uses the latest innovations in learning techniques to provide comprehensive skills development and leadership training to every professional. Another priority for the firm is increasing diversity and developing women leaders. Deloitte's programs, including its Initiative for the Retention and Advancement of Women, are known as industry benchmarks for creating an inclusive culture and harnessing the varied backgrounds and experiences of a diverse workforce. The firm also formed a Gen Y Council to open dialogue about how different generations interact in the workplace and to serve as a sounding board on major programs.

These initiatives are dynamic additions to an organization that is consistently ranked among the best places to work by *Fortune, Crain's Chicago Business, The Chicago Tribune, The Wall Street Journal* and *BusinessWeek*.

"We view the business skills and experiences of our people as our greatest assets. They are what we have to offer our clients and give us a competitive advantage in the marketplace," said DeHaas. "In order to attract and retain the best talent, Deloitte is committed to recruiting from the top schools across the country and building a workplace culture that allows our people to create satisfying careers and continuously increase their value as professionals."

It has been more than a century since William Welch Deloitte opened his accountancy office in London, laying the foundation for the organization known today for providing valuable and trusted advice to corporations around the world. From its humble beginnings to the present, the firm has been led by many extraordinary men and women who have shaped its culture of excellence and innovation, pushed it to meet the highest standards and made sure it was woven into the fabric of the communities in which it practiced. These core values have served the organization well and are sure to produce the next generation of leaders who will spur Deloitte to even greater heights over the next 100 years.

As used in this document, "Deloitte" means Deloitte LLP and its subsidiaries. Please see www.deloitte.com/us/about for a detailed description of the legal structure of Deloitte LLP and its subsidiaries.

of Consequence Luncheon. As someone who attended Club events in the past, she expressed her excitement about joining The Club in its centennial year. "The opportunity to lead this venerable forum forward is a privilege I'm extremely honored to have and enthusiastic to advance with the members of The Executives' Club," said Bean.

Before Bean served up closing remarks, Maria Wynne, Chief Executive Officer of the Girl Scouts of Greater Chicago and Northwest Indiana, moderated an afternoon session titled, "Mentorship: Inviting Other Women to the Club," with panel members that included Nuria Fernandez, Senior Vice President of CH2M Hill; Ann Marie Goddard, Lead Partner, International Executive Services and KPMG's Networking of Women, at KPMG; and Jane Thompson, President of Wal-Mart Financial Services.

Earlier in the afternoon, Christie Hefner, Director of the Center for American Progress, led an enlightening chat with Katie Burke Mitic, Director, Platform and Mobile Marketing at Facebook, and Ellen Levy, Vice President of Strategic Initiatives at LinkedIn. An audience of women and men gladly silenced their smart phones for this give-and-take on social media and the benefits of building a powerful network of business associates.

With all there was for guests to take in at the Women's Leadership Centennial Summit, Lagarde's luncheon address and Maggie Daley's surprise appearance seemed to funnel the day's collection of conversations into one. It's safe to say that Lagarde's rise to finance minister of France put her at the heart of the global response to the 2008 financial meltdown and the Euro crisis. In the International North Ballroom, in a talk that came three months before she would be voted to the post of managing director of the International Monetary Fund (IMF)—the first woman to run the global financial institution—Lagarde delighted her audience by making it clear she was here to deliver a Chicago speech.

She began by reflecting on all that has changed since she was a Board member of The Executives' Club, noting her pride in seeing a Chicago resident elected president and the Chicago Bulls return to the playoffs. With the theme of balance and imbalance, she spoke of

In accepting The Club's distinguished International Executive of the Year Award, Glenn Tilton, Chairman of the Board of United Continental Holdings, Inc., served up a luncheon address titled, "Competitive Realities in the Global Marketplace."

banking and market reforms and the resolve of the French government to continue to work closely with other nations in the recovery effort. Punctuating her address with sharp wit, she promoted the perspectives of women, warned of the temptations of protectionism, and encapsulated the issues to be discussed at the G20 Summit in France later in the year.

In drawing to a close, she recalled her very first visit to Chicago. She was a college student visiting from her native France. Before her tour of the U.S. by Greyhound bus landed her in the city, American friends had advised her it was a dangerous place. When the bus did make its stop in Chicago, she heeded their warnings and chose to stay onboard.

But, she came to know a different city when she returned in 1999 to serve as the global leader of Baker & McKenzie. With a nod to Daley, Lagarde described this renewed city as one that inspires confidence in the future. "I thank Chicago for demonstrating to the world that there is a path to reinventing oneself," she said. "It has not happened randomly. It has happened because of the sheer will, the leadership, the enthusiasm, the dedication, and the commitment of all Chicagoans."

STRENGTHENED BY THE SPIRIT OF COLLECTIVE LEADERSHIP

It was in the early 2000s that a group of female members of The Club began expressing the need for a program that speaks more directly to the interests and concerns of professional women. Terry Savage and Deb DeHaas were among those who began drawing up a blueprint of such a program, and the quarterly Women's Leadership Breakfast Series is now Chicago's largest speakers' forum of its kind.

"I still remember sitting at a restaurant somewhere on the North Side with a small group of women leaders," said Deb DeHaas, Vice Chairman and Central Region Managing Partner at Deloitte LLP, and a Board member of The Club since 2000. "We were sharing ideas and literally writing them on napkins and pieces of paper at the table."

After spending time shaping the format, frequency, and featured themes of the program, the group received the enthusiastic blessing of other Board members to carry forward with their plans. On September 21, 2004, the Women's Leadership Series was launched with a program titled, "Personal Risk Taking: How Much Should One Put on the Line." During the discussion, panelists shared their strategies and experiences on successful risk taking—including when and how to challenge the status quo, how to promote and advance new ideas, and how to be a forerunner for change.

In the years since, the program has continued to grow in popularity and now typically attracts more than 1,000 attendees—primarily women— to breakfast events organized around a theme relevant to women from diverse fields. Its speakers and panelists include role models of success equipped to share lessons of value to women at varying stages of their career. It's this program that inspired the Women's Leadership Centennial Summit.

"I think many of us have chosen to get involved and stay involved because we have recognized how important it was for us to have women who helped us along," said Sharon Oberlander, Senior Vice President, Investments at Merrill Lynch and Co-Chair

Richard C. Vie, Chairman Emeritus of Kemper Corporation, served as Chairman of The Executives' Club in its 2007–2008 season.

of the Women's Leadership Series. "We have a strong commitment to providing support to the next generation of women leaders."

"My firm has been a strong supporter of this series since its inception," added Kimberly Simios, Ernst & Young Assurance partner and Co-Chair of the Women's Leadership Series. "It's been an incredibly rewarding experience to bring together a group of professionals who understand the joys and challenges of a successful career, and support each other on a regular basis. Through this program, I believe we've done a great job of promoting the power of inclusiveness and gender equity, while also showcasing the unique perspectives of women leaders."

As for DeHaas, she also contributed to the foundation of another program of The Club that's designed to impart seasoned knowledge to future leaders. Over the years, the Chicago CEO Breakfast Series has introduced the Chicago business community to many CEOs who have taken the helm of multinational corporations headquartered in the metropolitan area as well as those who have recently relocated their companies here.

Glenn Tilton was one of the program's distinguished speakers after coming to Chicago in 2002 to become President and CEO of the Chicago-based UAL Corporation and Chairman and CEO of United Air Lines, its principal subsidiary company at the time. In this Centennial year, at another of The Club's well-attended Centennial Signature Programs, he was honored as the International Executive of the Year. The Club's first International Executive of the Year Award, in 1995, went to Microsoft's Bill Gates.

It was in great part Tilton's leadership of the global airline that ultimately led to the company's high-profile merger with Continental Airlines, which formed the world's largest carrier. As Chairman of the Board of United Continental Holdings, Inc., the parent company of the combined airline, Tilton's address at the International Executive of the Year Luncheon on April 26th centered on "Competitive Realities in the Global Marketplace."

With more than 1,000 businessmen and women filling the room, Tilton talked of the strength and expanded reach of the new United and the new jobs it is bringing to the Chicago area. At a time of rising fuel prices and state taxes, however, he also stressed that government at every level must work cooperatively with business for companies in his industry and others to remain globally competitive. "The global marketplace is only going to get more complex and more challenging," he said.

Whether it is Glenn Tilton, Christine Lagarde, Jeffrey Immelt or the many others who have graced its stage, The Executives' Club's consistency in featuring speakers proven in their leadership and outspoken in their beliefs has reinforced its brand again and again.

As Chairman of The Club's 45-member Board of Directors in the first half of this centennial year, Craig Donohue has worked with Board members and The Club's tireless staff to shape the season's programming. Donohue attended events of The Executives' Club for several years, and became more formally involved in the organization when he was asked to join its Board in 2005. Named CEO of the CME Group in 2004, he was instrumental in the 2007 acquisition that merged the Chicago Mercantile Exchange

UNITED CONTINENTAL HOLDINGS

On April 6, 1926, a Swallow biplane carrying U.S. mail touched down in Boise, Idaho, and continued on to Elko, Nevada—marking the first flight for Varney Air Lines and putting history in motion for both United and Continental. While Varney Air Lines went on to become United, its founder, Walter T. Varney, later established Varney Speed Lines, which eventually transformed into Continental.

A year after that first flight, airplane pioneer William Boeing founded his own airline, Boeing Air Transport, and began buying other airmail carriers, including Varney. In March 1928, the new United Aircraft & Transport Corporation began providing coast-to-coast passenger and mail service. It took 27 hours to fly the route, one way.

In 1930, as the airlines began to take on more passengers, Boeing Air Transport hired registered nurse Ellen Church to assist passengers. Prior to this, the only airline cabin attendants were male. Church is now known for being the first stewardess to take to the skies.

Flying cross-country in a day seems like a breeze today. But it wasn't until 1933, when United introduced the Boeing 247, that passengers could fly across the U.S. without an overnight stop or changing planes for the first time.

United's early route system operated east-to-west along a transcontinental route from New York City via Chicago and Salt Lake City to San Francisco, as well as north-and-south along the West Coast. The early interconnections during this era became the basis of major United hubs in Chicago and San Francisco, followed later by Denver and Washington, D.C. These four cities remain United hubs to this day.

While business declined during the Depression, World War II provided an opportunity for United-trained ground crews to modify airplanes for use as bombers, and transported mail, material, and passengers in support of the war effort. Post-war United benefited from both the wartime development of new airplane technologies (like the pressurized cabin which permitted planes to fly above the weather) and a boom in customer demand for air travel.

At the end of WWII, airlines began using jet-powered aircraft and by 1961 United had the world's largest jet fleet. That same year, United displaced American as the world's second largest airline. In 1968, the company reorganized, creating UAL Corporation, with United Airlines as a wholly owned subsidiary.

The 1980s were an exciting decade for the airline. In May 1981, United launched its MileagePlus loyalty program. In the following year, United became the launch carrier for the Boeing 767. United hit another milestone in 1984 when it became the first airline to serve all 50 states by introducing service to Atlanta, Nashville, Memphis, Little Rock, Fargo, Casper, Jackson, and Charleston.

In 1983, United gained its first overseas route and began operating flights to Tokyo from Portland and Seattle. Just two years later, United decided to purchase Pan American World Airways' entire Pacific Division, aircraft, and flight crew. And just three years after its first overseas route, United operated flights to 13 Pacific destinations.

The excitement continued through the turn of the century. In 1997, United co-founded the Star Alliance with Air Canada, Lufthansa, Scandinavian Airlines, and Thai Airways. That same year, United opened a major hub at Los Angeles International Airport. After becoming the launch carrier for the Boeing 767 in the '80s, United continued this tradition by becoming the launch customer of the Boeing 777. It was also the first airline to introduce the twin-jet in commercial service.

In May of 2010, Continental and United announced their intent to combine in a merger of equals. On October 1 of the same year, the companies legally closed their merger and became subsidiaries of the holding company, United Continental Holdings, Inc. The new airline combines the best assets of each company to create the world's leading airline.

Now more than a year into the integration process, the new United has made great progress. The two airlines share common management, and are part of the same team, working across two companies. However, Continental and United will continue to operate as separate airlines until they receive a single operating certificate from the FAA.

Every day, the United and Continental subsidiaries, along with their regional partners, launch nearly 6,000 flights to more than 370 airports around the world from hubs in Chicago, Cleveland, Denver, Guam, Houston, Los Angeles, New York/Newark Liberty, San Francisco, Tokyo and Washington, D.C.

United is taking the synergies from the merger and investing it back into its product, technology, fleet, facilities, and co-workers. The carrier is investing more than $550 million in onboard improvements, and will be the North American launch customer for the game-changing Boeing 787 Dreamliner aircraft in 2012.

The company has adopted a Working Together culture based on dignity and respect and direct, open and honest communication. United is focused on becoming the company customers want to fly, co-workers want to work for, and shareholders want to invest in.

(CME) with The Chicago Board of Trade (CBOT), which in essence established the CME Group, as well as the company's acquisition of the New York Merchants' Exchange (NYMEX) in 2008. As the leader of a company whose combined heritage spans more than 150 years, Donohue sees the strength of such staying power in relatively simple terms.

"Just like CME Group, I think The Executives' Club has really thrived on the quality of its product, which is made up of programs that bring Chicago business leaders and civic leaders together," said Donohue, who was honored as The Club's 2009 International Executive of Year. "But there has also been continued innovation. One of the hallmarks of The Executives' Club has been its ability to develop new programming and cultivate new members over many decades."

At The Executives' Club, those who rise to Chairman begin as Board members and serve as Second Vice Chairman and First Vice Chairman before beginning their term at the top. David Nelms, Chairman and CEO of Discover Financial Services, who was the First Vice Chairman, was elected Chairman in the second half of the centennial year. Ilene Gordon, Chairman, President and CEO of Corn Products International, Inc., was elected Second Vice Chairman.

Richard C. Vie, Chairman Emeritus of Kemper Corporation, formerly Unitrin, Inc., is a long time member of The Club and was its Chairman in 2007–2008. "You get a good sense of the organization by serving on the Board, and the chair positions further your understanding of how things work and what your responsibilities are by the time you become Chairman," said Vie.

The consecutive seasons of Vie's term were, from an attendance standpoint, among the most successful in the organization's history. "Timing is everything," he said with a laugh. In fact, The Club's speakers during his chairmanship included William Wrigley, Jr., while the famed company that he led was in the midst of change, and Sam Zell, who at the time had just sold Equity Office Properties and was quietly considering the prospects of purchasing the Tribune Company. "The big news that day was Sam Zell had on a coat and tie," said Vie. "The most memorable and rewarding aspects of being Chairman are getting to work with outstanding businessmen and women and working closely with The Club's staff. It's really quite a privilege to be Chairman, because if you look at the list of past chairmen of The Club you're looking at truly great leaders of Chicago business."

Before speakers take the podium at the events of The Executives' Club, connections and conversations at the table are already underway.

From its corporate base in suburban Westchester, Corn Products International has grown into a multinational organization that makes foods more available on a global scale.

CORN PRODUCTS INTERNATIONAL

Though it may not be recognized as a household name, for more than 100 years Corn Products International, Inc. (NYSE: CPO) has helped set the table for millions of households around the world. An industry leader in developing innovative food ingredients that make foods more available and affordable on a global scale, the company provides ingredient solutions to industries that include beverage, pharmaceutical, corrugating, animal feed, and health and wellness. From making foods and beverages taste better and baby powders and cosmetics smoother to the touch to providing ingredients used in IV solutions, Corn Products is a key ingredient in products that people depend on every day.

Headquartered in the Chicago suburb of Westchester, this company's largest plant was born in the city's Bedford Park neighborhood in 1906 at the dawn of the modern corn refining industry. In fact, the neighborhood is named after the founder of Corn Products, Mr. E.T. Bedford.

In the early 1900s, Corn Products Refining Company, as it was known, had already expanded into European markets and by the mid-1920s, after receiving a patent for crystalline dextrose, the company established refining operations in Argentina, Brazil, and Mexico. In the decades since, the company has continued its global advance in becoming a leading global ingredient provider to the food, beverage, brewing and pharmaceuticals industries as well as numerous industrial sectors.

In recent years, Corn Products further strengthened its multinational leadership positions through strategic alliances and acquisitions, key infrastructure and capital expansions, innovative ingredient development, and impressive financial performance. The company currently employs approximately 10,000 people in North America, South America, Europe, the Middle East, Africa, Asia and Australia. Through company-owned operations, joint ventures, alliances and technical licenses, Corn Products has 48 plants spanning 20 countries, and has sales and research and ingredient development centers in key global markets.

"We have a long history of meeting the changing needs of our customers," said Ilene Gordon, Chairman, President and Chief Executive Officer of Corn Products since 2009. "Our regional businesses, staffed by experts who understand the unique needs of their specific markets, are supported by a global network of engineering and ingredient development professionals that create innovative solutions for our customers around the world."

Charting a corporate history that parallels Chicago's growth as an international business center, Corn Products has enjoyed a competitive advantage in the industries it serves. "With its strong business and cultural institutions as well as institutions of higher education, Chicago is a great source of people with the skills and talent to help drive a company's successful growth," said Gordon. "At Corn Products, leadership development and succession planning is an ongoing priority. Anybody can buy machinery, but it is people that make the difference in our ability to create value for our customers around the world."

1940–1960

RECOGNIZING THE ROLE OF PROGRESS AND PIONEERS

When the president of a Chicago ice company became Chairman of The Club in June of 1940, his introductory address to members included a carefree slice of humor. "Frankly, I have at this time no conception of any rigid routine or set program which I may now recommend to you, but, on the contrary, I may perhaps be like the blind man in the nudist colony and just sort of feel my way along."

Harold O. McLain may have only been looking for an early laugh from the crowd, but his hint of openness about the future, it turns out, served him and The Club well. It was during his two-year term that the country adjusted to another war, and The Club's programming in many ways became a platform for the conversations surrounding it. Like other early leaders, McLain's title was actually President of The Club, but his role was equivalent to the Chairman position of today.

While more politicians, journalists, and military leaders would be added to its slate of active leaders and business supporters, The Club had already become a campaign stop for Midwest politicos like Everett M. Dirksen. Dirksen represented the 16th Congressional District of Illinois when he outlined the priorities of Congress at The Club in February of 1940. He would later become a U.S. Senator and, among other accomplishments, help write the Civil Rights Act of 1964.

It was Colonel Robert R. McCormick, the Editor and Publisher of the *Chicago Tribune,* who illustrated the political divide that existed before World War II when he addressed The Club three months later. Though his remarks referenced Al Capone and John Dillinger among other local concerns, McCormick zeroed in on President Franklin D. Roosevelt and his New Deal response to the Great Depression. Challenging his audience to examine the consequences, he said, "How far are we from Hitlerism, or Leninism, or Mussoliniism, or New Dealism—they are all the same."

Raymond Moley, then former Secretary of State in the Roosevelt Administration, offered another perspective on the New Deal in his presentation at The Club on April 18, 1941, but the debates around economic policies and financial reform faded after the attack on Pearl Harbor and the U.S. entry into World War II.

On April 19, 1941, just 12 days after the attack, U.S. Senator Robert A. Taft of Ohio—the son of the man who held the Oval Office in the year The Club was founded—struck a chord of unity in the Ballroom at the Hotel Sherman. Chairman McLain also eloquently acknowledged the country's change in focus with his introductory remarks that day. "Today this nation is a compact, homogeneous unit devoted to the single, dominant objective of winning the war," he said. "All of our preceding differences of opinion, personal antagonism, bitterness and debate now must be and now properly are submerged in the one all important patriotic opportunity of doing something to help our country in its time of peril."

One of America's Outstanding Young Statesmen

The Executives' Club of Chicago

urges you to hear

THE HONORABLE

JOHN F. KENNEDY

UNITED STATES SENATOR
FROM MASSACHUSETTS

"UNITED STATES AND ASIA"

Friday, 12:00 noon, May

Grand Ballroom, HOTE

Not long ago President Eiser
of Southeast Asia to a row
The first one, he said, was
the rest would be knocked
domino teetered on edge. Di
Union resistance to Commu
F. Kennedy, brilliant Sena
his first term as a U. S. Se
for the American people
...ding Sen. Kennedy
...y of S
what
hould
of
thi

The Executives' Club of Chicago

is pleased to present

Harry S. Truman

Former President of the United States

Friday, *12:00 noon,* **September 9, 1955**

Grand Ballroom, Conrad Hilton Hotel

Former President of the United States Harry S. Truman, will open the 45th season of The Executives' Club of Chicago. Mr. Truman, who needs no introduction to our members, will speak on a subject of his own choosing.

Mr. Truman's appearance on our platform will mark his first major address since completing his memoirs which have filled his time since his retirement in Independe...

As 1956 draws nearer we anticipate with great inte... Mr. Truman's views on the political scene.

Our members are urged to get their reservations in ea... for this surely will be a sell-out meeting! Please note ... limitation on tickets.

Reuben A. Borsch,
President,
will preside

NOTE: It is necessary to limit
...ach member to a total of 3
...ckets. Due to the large ticket
...le no telephone reservation...

Grand Ballroom, CONRAD HILTON HOTEL
Friday, 12:00 noon, September 9, 1955
Harry S. Truman

PLEASE RESERVE ______ *plates for members* } *$3.25 each, table of 10*
______ *plates for guests*

Enclosed is my check for total of $ ______

Send tickets to

The Executives' Club of Chicago

is honored to present

Richard M. Nixon

Vice President of the United States

Thursday, *12:00 noon,* **March 17, 1955**

Grand Ballroom, Conrad Hilton Hotel

Vice President Nixon, who needs no introduction to our members, will speak on a subject of his own choosing.

The young, personable Vice President who will make his first major address in Chicago since his election in 1952 will appear before us following an extensive good will trip throughout Central America.

We anticipate with great interest his views on world affairs at this time.

Our members are urged to get their reservations in early, for this surely will be a sell-out meeting! Please note that the meeting will be on Thursday noon instead of Friday.

Grand Ballroom, CONRAD HILTON HOTEL
... March 17, 1955

IN THIS ISSUE
"WHY HITLER CANNOT WIN"
by Dr. Gerhard Schacher

EXECUTIVES' CLUB NEWS

No. 41

June 12, 1942

Chicago, U. S. A.

FRIDAY (twelve) NOON
JUNE 12, 1942

HOTEL SHERMAN
GRAND BALL ROOM

SPECIAL

HUGO SPECK

Bureau Chief, Berlin Office—International News Service

Subject

"The Russian German Front"

JUST RETURNED LAST WEEK ON THE SWEDISH DIPLOMATIC EXCHANGE LINER — DROTTNINGHOLM — AFTER FIVE MONTHS INTERNMENT IN GERMANY STARTING LAST DECEMBER. MR. SPECK WAS RELEASED IN A PRISONER EXCHANGE AGREEMENT.

Hugo Speck is an experienced American newspaper man and has covered all the important cities and news fronts of Europe for the past eleven years.

He is a Texan by birth—was a student at Northwestern and a reporter for two years for the Chicago Tribune. During his time in Europe he became a specialist on the Balkans and has seen more of the Russian front from the German side than any other American reporter.

He started broadcasting over WLW in Cincinnati last Friday and has done practically no speaking in America since his return.

HERE'S YOUR OPPORTUNITY TO GET THE LATEST AND MOST AUTHENTIC FIRST HAND INFORMATION ABOUT THAT ALL IMPORTANT GERMAN RUSSIAN FRONT WHICH PROMISES TO HEADLINE THE NEWS THIS SUMMER.

ANNUAL ELECTION OF OFFICERS AND DIRECTORS
(Polls Open from 12:00 Noon to 12:35)

(While this is not a reservation meeting, we will be pleased to reserve space for those who have a party of four or more, on request.)

Luncheon, $1.00.

Tickets on sale at door.

June 19, 1942
ILLINOIS DAY
GOVERNOR DWIGHT H. GREEN WILL SPEAK
COLORED MOTION PICTURES—"THE OPEN ROAD."

IN THIS ISSUE
RADIO'S FAMOUS "QUIZ KIDS"

November 9, 1943

No. 17

RESERVATION MEETING

FRIDAY (twelve) NOON
NOVEMBER 12, 1943

MARSHALL FIELD III

Founder and Editor, The Chicago Sun

Subject

"Post-War Chicago"

THE NAME MARSHALL FIELD IS VIRTUALLY SYNONYMOUS WITH CHICAGO AND VOLUMES HAVE BEEN WRITTEN TO RECORD ITS CONTEMPORARY HISTORICAL BACKGROUND WITH THAT OF CHICAGO.

At the age of twelve Mr. Field lost both his father and grandfather. He was then known as "the richest boy in the world." His mother moved from Chicago to London in 1906 and young Marshall was sent to Eton and then to Cambridge. He returned to America in 1914 to take over the trusteeship of his grandfather's estate at the age of 21.

In 1917 Mr. Field enlisted in the Army as a private, ten days after the U. S. declared war. Appropriately as a champion horseman, he entered the cavalry, but went to France with the artillery (33rd division) where he made an excellent war record and was cited for bravery in action at St. Mihiel. He retired from the Army with the rank of Captain.

He organized the Chicago investment house of Field, Glore & Company and became engaged in numerous other business enterprises. In December, 1941, Mr. Field founded The Chicago Sun, with which you are all familiar, and on September 23, 1943, on his 50th birthday, he signed the documents bringing him into full control of his grandfather's immense estate.

Mr. Field deplores his inherited wealth and often remarks that if he cannot make himself worthy of three square meals a day, he doesn't deserve them. He is one of America's great philanthrophists and has done much to advance many of Chicago's worthiest charitable and civic enterprises.

In his talk to our club, Mr. Field will narrow down the post-war problem to its immediate effects on the citizenry of Chicagoland.

PRESIDENT MULROY WILL PRESIDE AND INTRODUCE THE SPEAKER.

Make Your Reservations Promptly on the Card Already Sent You.

Luncheon $1.25.

Tickets also on sale at door.

Friday, November 19, 1943
SPEAKER: Paul G. Hoffman
President of Studebaker Corporation,
Chairman, Committee for Economic Development.
SUBJECT: "Hey-day—A Signal for Action"
Reservation Meeting ($1.25)

In fact, Chicago's industrial base spurred a local war effort that boosted and remodeled its economy. Its aircraft plants alone employed 100,000 workers while other Chicago companies produced a range of components and field equipment for the military. All the while, of course, scientists at the University of Chicago, led by Enrico Fermi, were conducting research that contributed to the creation of the weapon that would ultimately end the war in 1945.

War bond campaigns were organized at The Executives' Club throughout the war and members were asked to bring a serviceman to events that included its Christmas party. The Club had the honor of hosting former President Herbert Hoover in December of 1942. Hoover examined "The Approaches to Peace." In November of 1943, as the Allies moved closer to victory, Marshall Field III spoke on "Post-War Chicago." Anticipating the challenges of the city's transition from a war economy to a peace economy, he cited Daniel Burnham's famous credo, "Make no little plans." Field concluded his address with this call to action: "As executives—as the doers of business—gentlemen, the future of Chicago is in your hands. Let us catch the vision of Dan Burnham and go ahead with Chicago now."

The Club responded by reaching out within the community to promote civic causes and programs and the city continued to build on its advances in research, technology, and industrial production. With the country at peace, The Club's inspiring speakers in the late 1940s and 1950s included Dale Carnegie, motion picture pioneers Cecil B. DeMille and Alfred Hithcock, and an actor and TV star named Ronald Reagan. The Ladies Day program on February 25, 1949 featured former First Lady Eleanor Roosevelt. Her granddaughter would participate in a Women's Leadership Breakfast in this centennial year, 62 years later.

The cloud of communism in the late 1940s, however, had seen DeMille address questions about the patriotism of those in his industry in his presentation before The Club in October of 1947. In June of 1954, Senator John F. Kennedy voiced more serious Cold War concerns when he warned of a potential expansion of the conflict in Indochina. By this time, The Club had already begun to invite area high school and college students to its meetings, and a group of them had a conversation with the Senator after his address. The same was true of Vice President Richard M. Nixon's visit to The Club a year later.

At the Kennedy address, Ward committeeman Richard J. Daley, a member of The Club, was among the other business and political dignitaries who sat at the head table with the young senator. A year later, as the city's new mayor, Daley would join Reuben A. Borsch, Chairman of The Executives' Club at the time, in greeting former President Harry S. Truman to Chicago at Midway Airport. Truman's keynote opened the 45th season of The Executives' Club.

With a revolving cast of illustrious speakers and presenters that included former and future Presidents, The Club certainly raised its profile and that of Chicago in the 1940s and '50s. With the support of an enduring mayor and a membership nearing 3,000, it would soon celebrate its 50th anniversary in grand fashion, and look back on a half-century of progress and accomplishments that its group of founders likely never imagined.

The Electronic Encyclopedia of Chicago—at www.encyclopedia.chicagohistory.org —served as an additional source for some historical elements of Chapter One and Two. The Electronic Encyclopedia of Chicago is a collaboration between the University of Chicago Press, the Chicago Historical Society, The Newberry Library, and Northwestern University.

KEMPER

As one of America's leading insurance providers, the Kemper family of companies specializes in property and casualty, life, health and accident insurance products for individuals. Kemper Corporation (NYSE: KMPR), formerly Unitrin, Inc., celebrated its new name on August 25, 2011 by ringing the opening bell at the New York Stock Exchange.

Kemper's Property and Casualty Insurance businesses include Kemper Preferred and Unitrin Specialty, which sell automobile, homeowners and other personal insurance and commercial automobile insurance through networks of independent agents, and Unitrin Direct, which sells automobile, homeowners and renters insurance directly to consumers or through affinity and employer-sponsored voluntary benefit programs. Kemper's Life and Health businesses consist of the Kemper Home Service Companies and Reserve National, which bring a high level of personalized products and services to underserved niches within the life and health insurance marketplace.

With over $8 billion in assets, Kemper employs more than 7,000 associates across its recognized brands and serves more than 6 million policyholders nationally. By organizing its operating companies around distinct customer segments, the Kemper family of companies remains attuned to its customers' needs and committed to providing straightforward, personalized products and services. Kemper's flagship insurance companies have been in business for more than 85 years and are among the industry's most trusted sources for consumer insurance.

The Chicago-based company has benefited from the strength of a seasoned management team led by Donald G. Southwell, Chairman, President and Chief Executive Officer. Richard C. Vie, a past chairman of The Executives' Club of Chicago, is Kemper's Chairman Emeritus.

With more than 7,000 associates, Kemper serves the insurance and financial needs of more than six million policyholders.

Craig J. Duchossois, Chief Executive Officer of The Duchossois Group Inc., was a young executive when he became a member of The Club. Having applied lessons from his involvement over the years to his own style of leadership, he now serves as an advisor to the New Leaders Circle Leadership Development Program.

CHAPTER THREE

DRIVEN BY THE POWER OF RELATIONSHIPS

It makes perfect sense that among those mingling at the reception before The Club's International Executive of the Year Luncheon was a healthy number of professionals in the aviation industry. After all, Glenn Tilton would soon accept a distinguished award for his global leadership of United and address the world-wide standing of the major airliners. For Thomas J. Riordan, Jr., however, aviation wasn't the only angle that drew him to this Centennial Season program in late April. Riordan recently completed 20 years of service as a helicopter pilot in the U.S. Marine Corps, but he attended the Luncheon as a student exploring the potential pathway of a new career.

In fact, as a fulltime MBA student at the University of Illinois at Chicago, Riordan was in the Grand Ballroom of The Hilton Chicago as part of a class project on networking. After a career that saw him fly worldwide missions in support of U.S. and allied forces, his tactical exuberance was employed in shaking hands and sharing information with others readying for the main event.

"Going back to school is part of my effort to transition to a business career," said Riordan, who grew up in suburban Bolingbrook and Downers Grove and now lives in Cary with his wife and three children. Through the UIC Liautaud Graduate School of Business, he has also attended other events of The Executives' Club. "Coming to these meetings as a student or a working professional, you really get a sense of the businesses and the opportunities in Chicago," said Riordan. "To actually meet people who could be of help to me in the future is a rare opportunity in itself."

Interestingly, it's the networking aspect of The Executives' Club that, in the throes of a dragging economy, has also drawn some former members back to The Club. Several years ago Ted Sojda found himself too busy to attend The Club's events and halted his membership. The real estate agent with Koenig & Strey responded to the recession by renewing his membership in an effort to expand his circle of contacts. "The Club

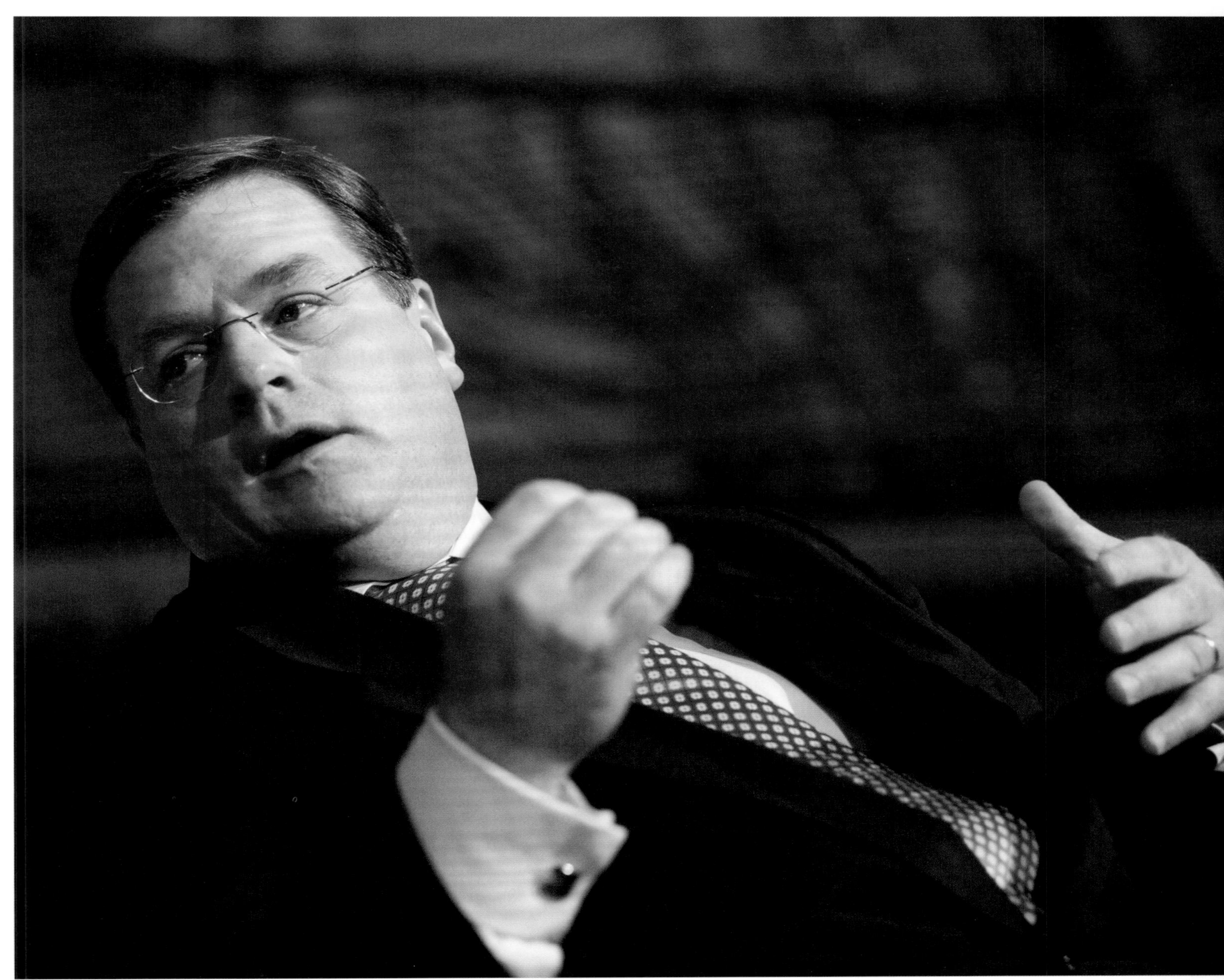

Gregory Case, President and CEO of Aon Corporation, discussed the elements and advantages of his company's recent merger at the Global Leaders Luncheon in May titled, "Risk & People: Two Big Issues, One Big Deal."

THE DUCHOSSOIS GROUP

Founded by Richard Duchossois in 1983, The Duchossois Group (TDG) is a family-owned company headquartered in Elmhurst, Illinois. TDG manages a number of diversified companies with a combined workforce of over 5,000 people and facilities in North America, Europe, and Asia.

A small corporate team provides strategic support, access to capital and an entrepreneurial spirit to the various companies that operate independently. In the past, TDG has reached beyond its own organization to both sharpen and share its management practices and strategies. TDG has been a member of The Executives' Club of Chicago since 1991.

"When we were first introduced to The Executives' Club, we saw the Board of Directors and the strength of its speakers' series provided an opportunity for our executives to learn from so many well respected global leaders," said Craig Duchossois, CEO of The Duchossois Group.

Today, Craig is a member of The Club's Board of Directors and a senior advisor to the organization's New Leaders Circle Development Program. "The opportunity for us to reciprocate later and provide leadership in nurturing potential future executives and bringing them together with community and global leaders is a priority," he said. "The New Leaders Circle makes a contribution to the future workforce and, in an increasing global marketplace, opening doors and welcoming new people and new opportunities. This is one of the many assets that make Chicago special."

As a complement to The Club's other pillars of programming, such as the Global Leaders Luncheons and the Women's Leadership Breakfast Series, the New Leaders Circle is also an asset to current corporate leaders. "One of the biggest fears of any CEO is getting disconnected, whether from the market, your employees, or the community," said Duchossois. "This interaction with young leaders gives CEOs a fresh and entrepreneurial perspective that can enhance their own leadership."

Leading a company with a global outlook, Duchossois views The Executives' Club as a gathering place for people and ideas that fosters a better understanding of the rest of the world. That The Club reflects the unique characteristics of Chicago has helped establish the organization's international spirit. "We're a city that has a great sense of community and of pride, but also a great deal of humility and a willingness to welcome people into our home," Duchossois said. "With this foundation in the years ahead, I think we're going to become even more internationally recognized as the place to meet new people, learn from many different types of leaders, and recruit outstanding young executives."

The history of The Duchossois Group can be traced back to a small rail car repair facility in the south suburbs of Chicago. Founded in 1916 by A.J. Thrall as the Union Wagon Company, the firm sold used and reconditioned rail car components.

keeps you connected with the business community and with individuals who are making changes to adapt to the times," he said. "When the economy is not cooperating, it's always smart to strengthen your professional network."

Rafael Martinez shares the same philosophy. When he worked for a company with a corporate membership to The Club, he became a regular at its many events. After a few years at The Club, he took a job with a company without a Club membership. Martinez chose to continue his involvement with a personal membership.

Sitting at a table before the start of a Global Leaders Luncheon in May titled, "Risk & People: Two Big Issues, One Big Deal," Martinez said he didn't want to lose ties with members he had gotten to know. As Gregory Case, President and CEO of Aon Corporation, and Russell P. Fradin, Former Chairman and CEO of AON Hewitt, took the stage that day to discuss the merger that brought their companies together, Martinez whispered, "Plus, where else can you have lunch with other business people and hear leaders like this talk casually about their company and their industry."

A GATHERING PLACE OF CONNECTIONS AND CONVERSATIONS

Networking has certainly been a core value of The Club since its foundation. With young leaders like Martinez and aspiring leaders like Riordan in mind, The Club added the New Leaders Circle Leadership Development Program to its pillars of programming in 2004 to enhance the connections it helps create among its up-and-coming members.

Designed to serve Club members who are 40 or younger and demonstrate leadership qualities and an accelerated career path, the New Leaders Circle cultivates their emergence through quarterly leadership development programs and a unique group mentoring program that provides them with extraordinary access to Chicago's senior executives.

"The concept was to reach further into our organization and help high potential future executives network as a group and offer them customized programming that includes interaction with some of the global leaders who visit our wonderful city," said Craig J. Duchossois, who is among a select stable of advisors to the New Leaders Circle.

As Chief Executive Officer of The Duchossois Group Inc., and a longtime member of The Club's Board, Duchossois knows well the benefits of information sharing at every level of business. A young executive when he joined The Executives' Club, his own leadership style was informed by his early involvement with The Club and its members. To serve as an experienced guide to the New Leaders Circle was an opportunity he couldn't pass up.

"This program not only assimilates new talent and new assets into the community, it provides the more senior executives with some very solid potential recruits for their own organizations," Duchossois said. "There are many points that I have picked up that I think have made me a better executive in providing leadership for our company."

Roger Crockett, President of R.O. Crockett Leadership, moderated a New Leaders Circle Leadership Development Program titled, "Thriving in the Global Economy through Reinventing Yourself."

In April of this centennial year, the New Leaders Circle Leadership Development Program was titled, "Thriving in the Global Economy through Reinventing Yourself." Held at the CME Group, the conversation was led by Roger Crockett, President of R.O. Crockett Leadership and an award-winning business writer who has interviewed leaders ranging from Procter & Gamble CEO Bob McDonald to Groupon chief Andrew Mason. Panelists Ginny Clarke, CEO & President of Talent Optimization Partners, LLC, Josh Schafer, Vice President of Global Oncology Strategy at Astellas Pharmaceuticals, and Yves Thill, Principal at A.T. Kearney, shared aspects of their business success and the personal and organizational transformations that have helped broaden their business perspective.

With companies of all varieties striking a global posture in today's marketplace, it's the grist of conversations like these that Duchossois sees as invaluable to leaders working to strengthen their business positioning. "Most of us have operations outside of the U.S., which means it's important not to be insular in your view of the business landscape," he said. "The New Leaders Circle and many other programs of The Executives' Club integrate a better understanding of international markets and different business cultures."

The Club's embrace of global thinking and international perspectives parallels Chicago's growth beyond its roots as a central hub for commerce in the U.S. "It has been and will continue to be a wonderful silo that gives Chicago a competitive edge over many other cities," said Duchossois.

In 2010, Chicago moved up two slots from the previous year to sixth in a ranking of global cities by *Foreign Policy* magazine, the management consulting firm of A.T. Kearney, and the Chicago Council on Global Affairs. The organizations analyzed data that included the number of major company headquarters, embassies, think tanks, political organizations, and museums as well as the flow of goods through airports and ports.

This point of progress isn't lost on Martin Slark, the Vice Chairman and Chief Executive Officer at Molex Incorporated and a Board member of The Executives' Club. Born and raised in the United Kingdom, Slark has spent much of his 35-year career at Molex building and overseeing the company's overseas operations. "If you grow up in Europe or spend time in Asia and look back at the United States, the industry of the East Coast or the technology of the West Coast tends to get the most attention," he says. "People often overlook the global reach of the companies that are based in Chicago and of the people that are based here. The Executives' Club has helped change that perception by showcasing what a truly global city Chicago continues to be."

Since 2005, Slark has been at the helm of a corporation with manufacturing locations in 16 countries. From its headquarters in suburban Lisle, Molex is a technology leader

After developing the plastic molding material called "molex" in 1938, the company's founder used its unique properties to solve customer problems.

MOLEX INCORPORATED

With the steady flow of data and devices in the hi tech marketplace continuing to reshape the everyday lives of people and businesses around the world, Molex Incorporated remains focused on meeting changing needs by breaking new ground. "As a company that makes the electronic components that go into many of today's electrical devices, we're excited about where the electronics industry is going and all the opportunities that creates," said Martin P Slark, Vice Chairman and Chief Executive Officer of Molex. "The pace of that change means we have to be continuously ready to respond to those opportunities."

Today Molex has a team of more than 35,000 employees in 40 countries with 39 manufacturing plants in 16 of those countries. Molex designs and manufactures more than 100,000 products serving original equipment manufacturers (OEMs) in industries that include automotive, data products, consumer electronics, business equipment, industrial automation, medical equipment, and telecommunications. Those products include everything from electrical and fiber optic interconnects to switches and application tooling, but the company's commitment to meeting customer needs on a local, regional and global level is still inspired by the development of a single proprietary plastic molding material, called "molex," in Brookfield, Illinois, back in 1938. Forming the molex material from limestone and waste by-products such as coal tar pitch, Frederick A. Krehbiel used it to design a variety of products, including flower pots, toys, salt tablet dispensers, clock cases, and insulators. Founding a company and aptly naming it Molex, Krehbiel and one of his sons, John H. Krehbiel, Sr., discovered novel ways to use the material's electrical insulating properties to solve customer problems. In 1945, Molex entered the electrical appliance market with a molded terminal block for the General Electric Hotpoint brand designed by John H. Krehbiel, Sr. By adding metal stamping to its molding processes, Molex manufactured its first connector for the appliance industry.

By the mid 50s, Molex began experimenting with other molding materials and expanding into new markets with products designed for different consumer and business applications. Over the years, the company's products appeared in washers, refrigerators, and electric stoves and later in vending machines, organs, and the newly introduced color television. After exploring printed and stamped circuitry, switching devices, and modular connections for printed circuit boards, Molex experimented with smaller, more powerful connections and launched its new high density "miniature" connector line to meet the needs of an evolving electronics industry.

Shifting its product focus to the computer, high-end telecom, and automotive markets, Molex began doing business in the global marketplace in 1967 and in 1970

With three global product divisions and a global network of design, engineering and manufacturing centers, Molex serves customers no matter where they are located.

became one of the first U.S.-based companies to open a manufacturing plant in Japan. In 1971, the company entered the European market with a plant in Ireland. It also became a public company in 1972 and opened its world headquarters on a 19-acre site in Lisle, Illinois, where it continues to operate from today.

"Our headquarters is no more than 10 miles from Brookfield, where the Krehbiel family started the company, so our entire 73-year history has unfolded here in the Chicago area," said Slark, who has held various positions in his 35 years at Molex. "From these roots, the culture of the company has been built around the concept of being loyal to the organization, being innovative and hardworking and having a comfortable and open communication style."

Having spent a significant part of his Molex career working in Europe and in Asia, Slark recognizes that for a company that operates dozens of plants around the world — including in China, Malaysia, Korea, Poland, Italy, Mexico, Thailand and Vietnam — fostering a singular organizational culture is hardly realistic. "We look at the common threads between us and try to mold the best ideas from the different geographies into more of a global culture," he said. "It takes a lot of communication and having cross-functional and cross-regional teams working on common challenges. If you look at any organization that has been successful for more than 70 years, you find that while those organizations may have to change how they operate on a global scale, they always maintain their core values."

Structured to support the company's worldwide reach, Molex consists of three global product divisions — Micro Products, Commercial Products and Integrated Products. Its global network of design, engineering, and manufacturing centers allows Molex to serve customers no matter where they are located. "I helped open Molex's first plant in China in 1984, so we have for a long time had a very global perspective," said Slark. "That perspective, which has also been encouraged by Chicago's image as an international city, has helped us prosper in a world that's become increasingly more global."

While close to 80% of the company's business today is outside of the U.S., Molex has continued to build on its history of supporting the Chicago community and its institutions. "Dating back to the company's founding, Molex has been a significant contributor to community initiatives and organizations," said Slark. "More importantly, our employees over the years have been active participants in those organizations. It's just part of being a good corporate citizen, and while we support all of the communities in which we operate around the world, Chicago has been a tremendous source of employees who have been the lifeblood of the company and the foundation of our success."

Increasing the diversity of Molex's workforce is just one priority of a company that, like many others, is positioning itself for the rising growth opportunities around the world. With economic forecasts of the next several decades projecting a great percentage of growth in Asia, the challenge involves leveraging existing strengths to support those opportunities. "For companies to succeed, particularly in the electronics industry, you have to learn how to operate in a truly global manner," said Slark. "Innovation drives our business, and our spending on combined capital expenditures and research and development is among the highest in the industry as a percent of sales. Relying on our people and our products, and guided by our history, we are uniquely well positioned to respond to new global opportunities by continuing to deliver successful solutions for our customers."

Two days after spinning-off from Morgan Stanley, in July of 2007, Discover Financial Services began trading on the New York Stock Exchange as an independent company.

DISCOVER FINANCIAL

The amount was $26.77, and the date September 17, 1985. This purchase, made in a Sears store in Atlanta by an employee from the Chicago area, marked the first transaction using a Discover card. Today, Discover is one of the most recognized brands in the U.S. and Discover Financial Services, headquartered in the Chicago suburb of Riverwoods, is a direct banking and payment services company employing more than 10,500 people in seven states and operating a global payments network that spans more than 185 countries and territories.

The modest purchase in Atlanta was part of an initial test-marketing program that would be followed by a national advertising campaign highlighted by the "Dawn of Discover" television commercial during Super Bowl XX. Together, these opening credits sparked the momentum of a company whose story of success has been shaped by bold ingenuity for the last 25 years.

Launched by Dean Witter Financial Services Group, Inc., a subsidiary of Sears, Roebuck and Co., Discover introduced itself to consumers with a promise of bringing change and innovation to the credit card industry. Focusing on features and services that consumers couldn't find in other credit cards, Discover pioneered cash rewards for purchases, no annual fee, and 24-hour live customer service. These customer-driven initiatives cut against the grain of a market dominated by two heavyweights of the industry.

It was in 1999, after Dean Witter, Discover & Co. merged with Morgan Stanley Group, that the card division was cast as Discover Financial Services. A year later, the bank that issues the Discover Card and has roots that date back to 1911 was renamed Discover Bank.

Despite being largely blocked out of the marketplace for payments transactions by Visa and MasterCard for much of its first two decades, the company broadened its sphere of services and continued to attract new customers by delivering unique product offerings with a personalized approach. The innovations that have complemented its array of services have included secure online account numbers, the industry's first keychain credit card, a biodegradable card, mobile banking applications for smart phones, and rewards cards designed for business, miles, and cash.

"When Discover was born, the aim was not just to introduce a credit card with more value to consumers and better service, but to offer additional direct banking services to consumers," said David W. Nelms, Chairman of the Board of Directors and Chief Executive Officer of Discover Financial Services. "Everyone said it was impossible to launch a new card and a new network from scratch. Hard work and a sense that we could accomplish anything was part of what made Discover successful in its early years."

The company's path to greater success was aided by a 2004 ruling by the U.S. Department of Justice in its case against Visa and MasterCard for anticompetitive practices. The ruling freed financial institutions like Discover to issue payment cards on competing networks and opened the door to increased choices for issuers, merchants, and consumers.

Discover became the first credit card services company to compete directly with Visa and MasterCard in the rapidly growing signature debit market when in 2005 it purchased the PULSE ATM-Debit Network and linked its more than 4,000 member banks, credit unions, and savings institutions with the Discover Network.

This strategic acquisition, along with the leveling of the network playing field, positioned the company to begin building a true global network. Discover also struck an

alliance with China UnionPay in 2005 that enabled merchants to accept Discover cards in China and UnionPay cards in the U.S. The following year, the company signed another reciprocal card acceptance agreement with JCB, the largest card issuer in Japan.

As Discover extended its reach around the world, it prepared for what is perhaps the most significant milestone in its young history. On July 2, 2007, two days after spinning-off from Morgan Stanley, Discover Financial Services began trading on the New York Stock Exchange as an independent company. "That was transformational for us," said Nelms. "Becoming a publicly-held, independent standalone company gave us in some ways a rebirth. We had been a very profitable company until then, but our independence allowed us to reinvest those profits into targeted aspects of our own business."

Discover took a formidable step in enhancing its capability to serve cardmembers anywhere in the world when it purchased Diners Club International in 2008. In acquiring this venerable financial institution, Discover added more than 185 countries and territories to its payment network. Established in 1950 in Chicago, Diners Club is credited with creating the first multipurpose charge card in the world. "Now that we've combined forces, you've got the newest network and the oldest network working together to really take on some very established competitors around the world, and doing so from Chicago," said Nelms.

In calling Chicago home, Discover has remained committed to supporting its global network with customer service centers based in the U.S. and staffed only by Discover employees. "We have our own system, our own network, our own brand," said Nelms. "Whether you're talking with one of our customer service representatives or interacting with us through our online system, communication is vital to our organization."

This commitment to the local communities it serves is also reflected in the company's passionate support of nonprofit organizations and charitable events and causes. In 2009 alone, Discover and its employees donated millions of dollars and provided more than 45,000 hours of volunteer time to more than 2,000 nonprofit organizations. In the Chicago area, Discover donated nearly $1 million to more than 80 nonprofit organizations. The company's relationship with Junior Achievement of Chicago has included providing employee volunteer teachers and financial support benefiting 22 schools and more than 1,900 students in communities throughout the area.

"Getting involved is a part of our culture and core values," said Nelms. "To our employees, I think the dollars are less important than the tangible acts of teaching young people or building a new playground at a school that really needs one."

Delivering tangible benefits to consumers is the impetus of Discover's products and services. In fact, it entered the student loan market at a time when a lot of other banks were withdrawing from it. The company's Discover Card cash rewards program, known as Cashback Bonus®, is now the leading program of its kind in the U.S. and Discover's business strategy has evolved into a mission toward becoming the country's largest direct banking and payment services company.

For Discover, charting the road ahead means remaining true to the ambitious nature of its beginnings. "The strategy of being the leader in direct banking domestically, as well as a leader in network payments globally, is something that we think has a lot of degrees of freedom," said Nelms. "It enables us to tie together our different lines of business and support a system that I think is the future of how people will conduct banking."

that delivers interconnect solutions for markets that include data communications, telecommunications, consumer electronics, industrial, automotive, medical, military, and lighting and solar. "I think I've always had a global view of the world and for any company to be successful in today's business climate they've got to operate on a global basis," said Slark. "I've been in meetings at The Executive's Club featuring leaders from India and China and many other countries around the world. It's through the forum of The Club that Chicago's business leaders, myself included, have gained a global scope on where their industry is headed."

Like a lot of The Club's Board members, Slark has articulated the strides and struggles of his company as a keynote speaker at its events. He admitted it is both daunting and edifying to discuss aspects of your own organization to a learned business audience. His first address, in fact, centered on Molex's efforts to reorganize its operations to be a more effective global company and the challenges the company faced through its transition. "The part I found particularly interesting was the question and answer session afterward because you get to hear what people in the audience are really interested in talking or learning about," Slark said. "It gives you an opportunity to more directly share your perspective with them."

For Slark and many other leaders of Chicago-based organizations, their overarching perspective often emphasizes the importance of a global outlook that is driven by the distinct advantages of local character. "To me, it's true that people of the Midwest are very open, very friendly, and very ambitious," said Slark. "Being from England and then having spent time in Asia and other parts of the world, I think the collective resolve and civic-minded environment of Chicago has a lot to do with the ongoing success of The Executives' Club. As an organization that has embodied those attributes, The Club has continued to foster the competitive advantages of Chicago and its business community."

ENGAGED IN A NEW AGE OF TECHNOLOGY

Whether it's Molex or Motorola, ITW or Navteq, companies and corporations that contribute to the rising tide of technology are by their very nature global enterprises. But as Slark contended, any company employing the tools of today's technology is in essence an organization with global reach. That access, of course, extends to consumers.

The early morning crowd at The Executives' Club's Centennial Technology Summit seemed to set their breakfast aside early as Scott Klososky launched into a presentation that powerfully illustrated the potential pitfalls of organizations unprepared to use technology to both protect and promote their reputation.

Klososky serves as the Founder and Chairman of the Board of Alkami Technology, a technology start-up that has developed a second-generation online banking platform. But his keen vision as a thought leader on emerging technologies and social networking

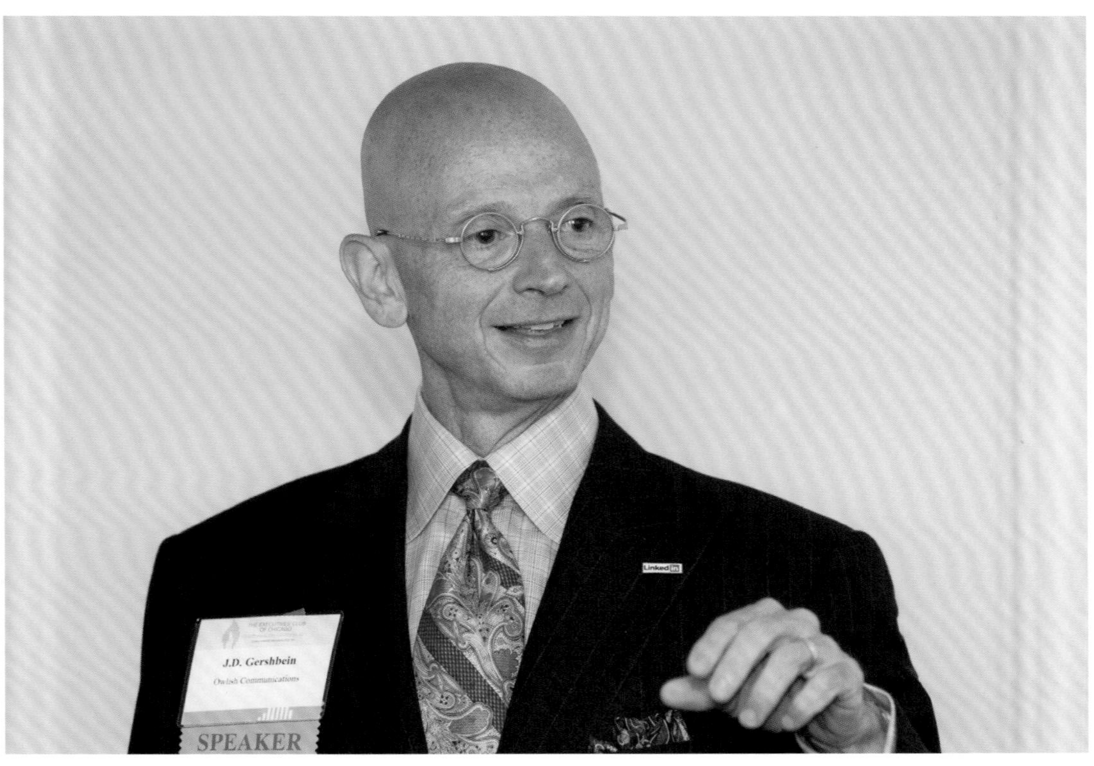

J.D. Gershbein, the CEO of Owlish Communications, was one of the tech savvy leaders at the Centennial Technology Summit, a day that was filled with, as it was titled, "Tech Tools and Tips to Maximize Your Personal Productivity."

has seen him travel the world as a speaker and business consultant. Klososky was one of several interactive experts espousing smart and savvy ideas at the Centennial Technology Summit.

The full day event at The Hilton Chicago was dubbed, "Tech Tools and Tips to Maximize Your Personal Productivity," and Klososky's morning eye-opener was titled, "Trends, Technology, and Taking the Lead." He took the lead with a big-screen review of unnerving and entertaining viral videos that reached audiences around the world with a few easy clicks. The videos included creative customer complaints against corporations as well as online corporate commercials that effectively complement their brand messaging in other mediums.

Klososky's message quickly became clear. Social media is a tool that has not only catapulted pre-teen crooners into overnight stars but has also elevated corporate missteps—both real and exaggerated—into a swell of public criticism. Organizations that engage in social media and proactively promote their corporate image and respond to issues that might damage it are able to stay ahead of a technological world that promises challenges and opportunities virtually everyday.

After the Summit's breakfast program, one of the day's breakout sessions put a firm focus on personal opportunities. J.D. Gershbein, the CEO of Owlish Communications, engaged his audience in a witty examination of social networking. "How many people have a LinkedIn account?" Gershbein queried the diverse group of men and women. "And how many have simply cut and pasted your resume into your LinkedIn profile?"

Seeing sites such as LinkedIn as a resource that not enough individuals and companies

Melissa L. Bean, President and CEO of The Executives' Club, is certainly among those who view the organization's events as an opportunity to network and share ideas.

have used to their best advantage, Gershbein founded his company to help them discover the possibilities. In his visual presentation, he demonstrated how professionals could distinguish themselves on the business-centered site and, if applicable, support the priorities of the companies they represent. He also delved into the etiquette of interaction in building a network of contacts, which includes serving as a credible connector between contacts. "If it's mutually beneficial for the people you bring together, it is beneficial to you as well," he advised.

The Centennial Technology Summit also featured a broader panel discussion on social media and other aspects of technology and innovation that can impact the bottom line. In the morning, some attendees of the event boarded a bus and were given a guided tour of the Microsoft Technology Center in Chicago and the CME Group's Global Command Center. Before the afternoon sessions, the Summit crowd convened in the hotel's International North Ballroom for an energizing Global Leaders Luncheon keynoted by Ursula Burns, the Chairman and CEO of Xerox Corporation.

The first African American woman to lead a Fortune 500 company, Burns related the inspiring chapters of her journey before addressing U.S. competitiveness and underlining the country's critical need to produce students steeped in the skills of science, engineering, and math. She spoke of her own daughter's incredible mathematical proficiency, and confessed that her daughter plans to be a creative writer. "It is important to follow your passion," she said with a smile.

Though egging laughs from the audience, Burns made clear her passion for nurturing young leaders hungry to make technology a focus of their future. After her talk, she posed for a picture with a Girl Scout Troop invited to the event.

It was perhaps fitting that David Nelms, in taking over The Club's Chairmanship position from Craig Donohue in the weeks leading up the Centennial Technology Summit, introduced Burns on a day that revolved around technological advances and opportunities. Technology has been at the forefront of Nelms' leadership at Discover, and he spoke about the company's process of expanding from a credit card network into a global financial services network at one of The Club's Technology Conferences in 2007. The Club actually started organizing Technology Conferences in 2001 to explore the evolving and increasingly complex issues of technology as both an industry sector and an innovation applied across industries.

"Today, every company is employing new technologies and adapting to the global marketplace," said Nelms, whose own company celebrated its 25th anniversary in 2011. "These periods of transition make the speakers and networking opportunities of The Executive's Club even more valuable to its members and guests. Part of the reason The Club has lasted so long is because it continues to adjust its programming to be relevant. Part of my role is to help build on that success."

Ursula Burns, the Chairman and CEO of Xerox Corporation, offered a stirring keynote address at a Global Leaders Luncheon that was built into the Centennial Technology Summit.

Right: A group of employees assembled for a photo in front of the Shakeproof division of ITW in 1939.

Far right: ITW's listing on the New York Stock Exchange in 1973 was a milestone celebrated by (left to right) Merle S. Wick, then vice president of the NYSE, and Silas S. Cathcart, then chairman of ITW, former chairman Harold B. Smith, Sr., and Harold B. Smith, Jr., president and CEO of ITW at the time.

ITW

In 1912, on the eve of World War I, Chicago financier Byron L. Smith placed an ad seeking an investment opportunity for "a growing manufacturing business." Four men answered: Frank W. England, Paul B. Goddard, Oscar T. Hogg and Carl G. Olson. Together, these forward-thinking businessmen formed a company to manufacture and sell metal-cutting tools. Nearly 100 years later, that company is a leading international business corporation that designs and manufactures an array of highly engineered fasteners and components, equipment and consumable systems, and specialty products and equipment for customers around the world.

At Illinois Tool Works (ITW), the recipe for success has focused on creating value-added advanced industrial technology products and making acquisitions that provide additional product solutions to its customers. Growing into a Fortune 200 company manufacturer, ITW now consists of decentralized business units in more than 50 countries and employs approximately 60,000 men and women. "For the great extent of our long history, we have operated with a decentralized environment that keeps our people close to our customers and markets," said David B. Speer, President, Chief Executive Officer, and Chairman of ITW. "With that structure proving effective over time, we have been successful in extending it globally without abandoning the processes and principles of our past."

In fact, it was Harold B. Smith, grandson of ITW founder Byron L. Smith, who as president of the company led the decentralization of ITW's operations in the 1940s to enhance its focus on specific markets. By this time, having already expanded its product line to support America's World War I effort, ITW was contributing to the country's World War II engagement with the development of a new timesaving wafer cutter to rifle heavy artillery barrels.

The company wasn't officially named Illinois Tool Works until its 50th anniversary in 1962, and its dynamic past is intertwined with the many companies it has established and acquired over the last half century. One of its earliest business units developed the Shakeproof twisted tooth lockwasher. That company, still going strong, operates its U.S. headquarters in Elgin, Illinois, not far from ITW's world headquarters in Glenview.

After establishing its name and becoming a member of the New York Stock Exchange in the 1960s, ITW increased its product developments for the construction industry and became the only company in the world to produce fastening systems for wood, metal, and concrete/masonry applications. On the global front, ITW acquired German components manufacturer Ateco, which provided Shakeproof and other products with better access to European markets. ITW also acquired W.A. Deutsher, an Australian company, to extend its reach into the region's construction, industrial, and packaging markets. In diversifying a portion of Shakeproof's capabilities in the late '60s, ITW formed a new business unit, Buildex, which became a leading supplier for the construction industry. It was in this era that ITW also transformed the beverage packaging industry when its new Hi-Cone operating unit invented the six-pack ring carrier.

In the 1970s, ITW and its partner companies spearheaded change with its manufacturing of components, fasteners, and assemblies for automotive companies around the world as well as with new capabilities providing sealants and other specialty chemical products used in industrial maintenance. In the following decade, it completed more than three-dozen acquisitions serving both existing and new markets. Chief among those was its purchase of Signode, a leading multinational manufacturer of metal and plastic strapping, stretch film, industrial tape, application equipment and related products. With this acquisition, ITW nearly doubled its revenues.

"We have always looked long and hard for acquisitions that we think fit inside of our business structure and fit with our growth strategies," said Speer, who joined ITW in 1978 and has held various selling, marketing, and general management responsibilities within the organization. "Innovation is a core element of any company we acquire, but the people within the company have to be a good fit as well. They have to be hands-on leaders who are comfortable operating in a decentralized fashion and comfortable driving change."

By 1990, the company had entered the finishing systems market with acquisitions of companies providing liquid and powder applications for conventional and electrostatic painting and its acquisitions continued to increase. In the '90s, ITW added nearly 100 companies to its portfolio, including DeVilbiss/Volstatic, Dynatec, Hobart Brothers Company, Miller Group, United Silicone, and Premark International. Its acquisition of Premark, a manufacturer of commercial food equipment and laminate products, marked the largest in ITW's history.

The company's proven strategies of increasing market penetration with product innovations, extending current products to new industries, and acquiring businesses that improve customer offerings has served as the foundation for its continued success in the 21st century. Complementing the entrepreneurial nature of its decentralized business structure, ITW follows an 80/20 business process built on the supposition that 80 percent of a company's sales are derived from the 20 percent of its product offering being sold to key customers. Applying this concept globally keeps the organization focused on its most profitable products and customers.

Since its early days, ITW has also maintained a focus on contributing to the growth and vibrancy of the city that has helped support its success. "There is great collaboration between the business, the civic, and the philanthropic communities of Chicago," said Speer. "We have certainly benefited from that network and, in being involved and invested in those communities, the rich fabric and resources of the Chicago area is very much a part of our organization."

Through its corporate giving program and the volunteer outreach of its employees, ITW continues to support a number of the city's community organizations and cultural institutions, from the United Way and Junior Achievement to the Chicago Symphony Orchestra. "It is a close-knit city, but with its world class companies in manufacturing, pharmaceuticals, and the financial services area, Chicago is certainly a global city," said Speer. "For its businesses and its people, Chicago serves as a vital connection to the global environment."

As ITW provides structure and guidance to so many companies in emerging markets around the world, the development of leadership to run those rapidly growing businesses is a critical priority. "Our leadership development programs are strongly based on mentoring," said Speer. "By attracting the right people and mentoring, coaching, and giving them the kind of development assignments that allow them to grow, our goal is to have the right people in the right place, at the right time."

With ITW approaching its centennial anniversary, the company's enduring success can be attributed to the skills of its people, the innovation of its products, and the strengths of its processes. "Our ability to effectively blend those elements has helped us achieve significant growth for many years," said Speer. "If we continue to identify and respond to customer needs by providing original, customized products and service, there's no question we'll continue to drive growth as we move forward."

1960–1980

CONTINUING A DIALOGUE THAT BRIDGES HISTORY

It's hard to believe that before John F. Kennedy was elected president The Executives' Club of Chicago had already celebrated 50 years of success. The Club marked the milestone with a Golden Anniversary Meeting on March 10, 1961 at the Hotel Sherman.

"I would like to take this opportunity to congratulate your officers and executive director, Art Stewart, for their effort in maintaining this noteworthy 50-year tradition of bringing busy executives together to partake of food for thought and nourishment through the medium of the luncheon forum," said Otto Kerner, the new governor of Illinois at the time and the day's featured speaker.

Mayor Daley was among the dignitaries who welcomed Kerner and the well-dressed crowd that filled the hotel's Grand Ballroom. The mayor also served as official cutter of the anniversary cake. The celebration came in the midst of a season that had begun with a roundtable presentation on troubled hotspots in the world by the foreign correspondents of NBC News and would soon see the popular mayor of West Berlin, Willy Brandt, pay a high-profile visit to The Club. The eclectic mix of speakers in 1961 ranged from former Vice President Richard Nixon to comedians Joey Bishop and Bob Newhart.

While humor had its place in the culture, the decade would ultimately be dominated by politics and peace marches, conflict and tragedy. On November 22, 1963, the audience that gathered to applaud the return of a noted Ohio congressman was stunned by the news that seeped through the Ballroom as he spoke. The Club's newsletter recounted the unfolding episode a week later.

The tragic shooting of President John F. Kennedy was learned by the guest speaker, Congressman Robert Taft, Jr., just as The Executives' Club meeting started on November 22. It was agreed by Judge Win G. Knoch of the U. S. Court of Appeals, who was presiding officer at the meeting, to go ahead with the meeting until rumors flying thick and fast could be confirmed. The audience was unaware of the shocking news.

The electrician in the control booth turned off the microphone and started to pipe a radio broadcast into the crowded ballroom just as the meeting was about to begin. After a couple minutes delay the microphone was turned on.

In the middle of Judge Knoch's introduction of the speaker's table, a guest at the table interrupted the Judge and informed the audience of the shooting. A few persons left the hall.

During the Congressman's speech the President's death was confirmed by the office staff and the speaker cut off the question period and Judge Knoch informed the audience. He asked that the 1200 members and guests stand in prayer. It was the saddest meeting in the 53-year history of The Executives' Club of Chicago.

The country, and The Club, carried on. Sticking to the tenor of its mission, The Club wasn't shy about presenting speakers who took on the complex and increasingly controversial issues of the day. A number of guests, on both sides of the debate, examined the country's policies in Vietnam. In fact, Secretary of Defense Robert S. McNamara was scheduled to speak at The Club in September of 1964.

is delighted to
for our Spring Ladies' Meeting

CONRAD HI

MARCH 19

reat

Program

SPECIAL TREAT!
DOUBLE QUARTET
FROM
AMHERST COLLEGE
WILL SING

RONALD REAGAN

Distinguished Actor and Television Star

After some years as a radio sports announcer, Ronald eagan, who has been described as "typically American as pple pie," signed his first motion picture contract, with arner Brothers, in 1937. Since then he has appeared in ore than 40 films.

He was president of Screen Actors Guild (1947-1952) and was drafted for a sixth term in 1959. Mr. Reagan is a member of the California Republican State Central Committee and has been mentioned prominently as a candidate for Governor of California.

His book "Where's the Rest of Me" will be out in April.

Be sure to hear Mr. Reagan and bring the ladies.

President, Harvey S. Olson, will preside.

BRING THE LADIES

Grand Ballroom

Friday, 12

Spring M

Please Re

Enclos

Sen

CZECHOSLOVAKIA
TORN BETWEEN TWO WORLDS

(The first complete UNCENSORED film on Czechoslovakia to reach the outside world—the most magnificent country behind the iron curtain)

DON SHAW

FRIDAY NOON, MARCH 3, 1961

TERRACE CASINO, MORRISON HOTEL

reatest scoop since World War II!
This is the only color-film ever made of Czechoslovakia as a Communist Satellite—completely uncensored!
Produced and presented by Don Shaw, in person, it is packed with up-to-minute views and news of life in a communist state, told for the first time. "Don Shaw's film is the kind of pulsating photography that draws you into the scenes for an intimate glimpse the life of Czechoslovakia's people today."
e Prague, Europe's most distinctive city; Pilsen, city of motor cars and beer; the resort areas of
e martyred village; and a festival at Domazlice. Meet the people and see the places of
on't miss this new, unusual, completely uncensored picture, filmed and

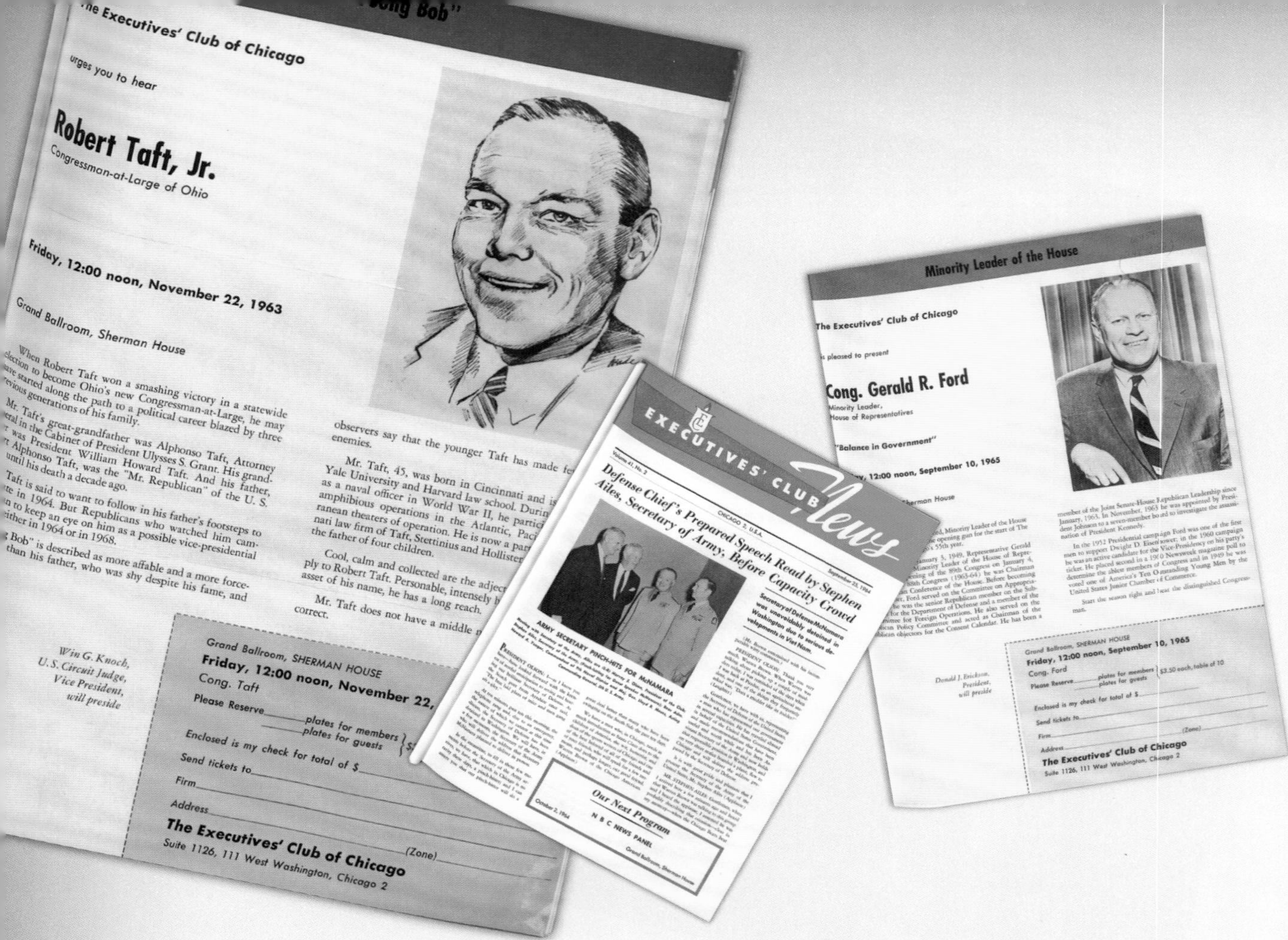

When an emergency related to the Vietnam conflict caused him to cancel his trip to Chicago, the Secretary of the Army arrived to read the Secretary's speech for him.

Congressman Gerald R. Ford opened The Club's 55th year in 1965 and Ronald Reagan returned to The Club for a ladies day event in March of that year. In his address, the actor not only exercised his well-known charm but also exposed his political character by blasting the government's economic policy at the time.

Even as the extenuating tensions of politics were stirring up divisions that would flare in the streets of Chicago in 1968, The Club also kept its eye on the economy, business, and education. From the Chairman of the Board of Governors of the Federal Reserve System and university presidents to a parade of corporate leaders—including Donald N. Frey of the Ford Motor Company, the Board Chairman of Honeywell, Inc., and Fred Broch, the President and Chairman of the General Electric Company—The Club kept its doors open to diverse perspectives. It also opened doors to potential future leaders when in 1964 it began offering college scholarships to area high school students.

In the years after the city hosted the Democratic National Convention, the turmoil of the times began to subside and Chicago was again being recognized for its strides as a business center—perhaps best symbolized by the opening of the world's tallest building in 1973, the Sears Tower. Change was also in the air at The Executives' Club in 1973, when the acting director of the FBI visited The Club to discuss adding women to the FBI ranks. Before the year was out, The Club began admitting women into its membership ranks. One of The Club's new female members in April of 1974 was a public relations representative for United Airlines and another was president of a Chicago-based company known as Intercomco International, Inc.

This historic step strengthened The Club's position as a preeminent leader of the Chicago business community, and The Club tightened its cohesive core with new membership receptions and social events that included a bowling league and theater trips. With a more diverse audience came more meetings devoted to business issues and more addresses by corporate visionaries like RCA Chairman Robert Sarnoff, who discussed the concept of satellite television, and H. Ross Perot, who chronicled the rise of his company, Electronic Data Systems.

Richard Nixon returned to The Club in 1974. With this visit, however, he became the first sitting President of the United States to address The Executives' Club. A few months later, on August 9, 1974, he would resign from office. Katherine Graham, the President and Publisher of the Washington Post Company, was among those who weighed in on the Watergate scandal at The Club.

As a forum for discussion about business and politics and cultural trends that ranged from war and peace to sports and religion, The Club was propelled by its ability to deliver insight in an era continually in search of logical perspective.

Whether it was General W.C. Westmoreland looking back on the lessons of Vietnam or Robert K. Wilmouth, the President and Chief Executive Officer of the Chicago Board of Trade, arguing for increased governmental support of free markets in the late 1970s, The Club voiced the importance of turning adversity into advantages and addressing challenges with action.

Challenges would indeed carry into the 1980s and beyond, and leadership in action would be key to reviving and reshaping The Club for a new generation.

THE PRIVATE BANK

The PrivateBank opened for business in 1991 in a vintage building at 10 N. Dearborn Street in Chicago. Known for its distinctive approach to private banking, the organization expanded by recruiting seasoned professionals committed to building client relationships and delivering exceptionally personalized service.

In 2007, The PrivateBank saw an opportunity to become Chicago's hometown, relationship-driven commercial bank, and to be a leading commercial bank in key Midwestern markets. The PrivateBank named Larry D. Richman President and Chief Executive Officer in November 2007 and in the following year added more than 150 Managing Directors with deep market knowledge to serve the needs of diverse middle market businesses by delivering products and services to the companies as well as their owners and executives. The bank places particular emphasis on serving commercial and industrial companies and commercial real estate developers, and has a legacy of excellence in private wealth services. Additionally, The PrivateBank continues to grow its community banking capabilities.

With the simple vision to be a top-performing, relationship-driven commercial middle market bank that is important to its clients and communities, The PrivateBank now operates 34 locations in 10 states and has operated as a public company traded on the NASDAQ Stock Exchange since 1999. The PrivateBank teams also value their communities, and contribute to the growth and success of cities and neighborhoods in and around Chicago through financial investment and volunteer service.

In carving out a unique competitive advantage in the Chicago marketplace, and concentrating on the specific needs of its well-defined clients, The PrivateBank is positioned for continued growth that will carry it into the future.

Carrying on a long tradition of cooperation and collaboration between The Executives' Club and City Hall, Mayor Rahm Emanuel made two appearances at The Club shortly after taking office.

CHAPTER FOUR

DRAWING CONNECTIONS AND PROMOTING PROGRESS

Catherine O'Connor hustles to the escalator on the lower level of the Fairmont Chicago. She's not alone. A casual stream of bright-faced men and women are funneling onto the steps moving upward to the hotel's main floor. Bits of conversation in the crowd allude to the stirring luncheon keynote address that has just wrapped up. It was O'Connor who introduced the luncheon speaker, and moderated a question and answer session with the well-known guest. On the escalator, she shifts one set of papers in her hands on top of another. Her fellow travelers are also headed to the next event of the day, and she is to serve as the introductory emcee of that meeting as well.

Focused, determined and personable, O'Connor has distinguished herself in her career at CDW and has emerged as a leading young member of The Executives' Club. At CDW, the Chicago-based provider of technology products whose success story includes it being considered one of the best U.S. companies to work for, O'Connor is the manager of enterprise servers and storage, a multi-billion dollar business unit. She heads a team of solution architects and collaborates with engineers in supporting the company's sales efforts.

At The Club, her involvement has grown in the last two years to include her current term as Chairman of the New Leaders Advisory Board. This Board contributes to the strategic direction of programs that appeal to aspiring leaders and its program committee helps develop and manage events that make up the New Leaders Circle Leadership Development Programs. "For the last year, our committee discussed program ideas that would meet the needs of up-and-coming leaders," O'Connor says while on her way from the escalator to a second floor conference room. "We think of events and speakers that will provide this audience with meaningful and actionable information."

In this centennial year of The Club, O'Connor's committee added to their efforts and designed a half-day event to standout as the New Leader's Centennial Summit. "Chicago's Got Talent: How to Have a Starring Role in Your Career" is all about helping new leaders discover the most desired skills in the marketplace and explore strategies to strengthen their individual value and enhance their personal brand. Its day has arrived, and O'Connor's role is to help manage the action.

The luncheon keynote she introduced to kick-off the event was served up by Harry Kraemer. A former Chairman and Chief Executive Officer of Baxter International Inc., Kraemer is an executive partner with Madison Dearborn, a private equity firm based in Chicago. He is also a clinical professor of management and strategy at Northwestern University's Kellogg School of Management.

In an address on "Values Based Leadership" that reflected the theme of his recently released book, *From Values to Action: The Four Principles of Values-Based Leadership,* Kraemer comfortably wandered the stage to engage each corner of the room. Displaying warmth, humor and authentic business acumen, he challenged young leaders to put humility and common sense at the center of their pursuits. "Take time to think," he advised. "All leadership starts with self-reflection." With O'Connor facilitating the question and answer session that followed, Kraemer thoughtfully applied his principles to specific queries from the crowd.

Now outside the busy doorway of the second floor conference room, which is filling up with many of those who attended the Kraemer address, O'Connor pauses to absorb the atmosphere. "This is why The Executives' Club is so good," she says. "Its ability to bring people together like this, and to share the wisdom of people like Harry, that's what really sets it apart."

The second of five career-based presentations planned for this day is about to begin. O'Connor glances down at the papers she's been carrying. Looking back up, she strides toward the podium to make another introduction.

WILLIAM BLAIR & COMPANY

Launching a new investment business in the wake of the 1929 stock market crash was fraught with risk, but William Blair recognized a window of opportunity when he and Frank Bonner opened William Blair & Company in Chicago in January of 1935.

Aware of the excesses and shoddy practices that had plagued his profession, Blair sought to establish a firm based upon the highest standards. In offering investment advice and raising corporate capital, the firm helped finance the growth of such companies as Household Finance Corporation, Continental Casualty and Continental Assurance companies (now CNA Insurance). These and other achievements spawned more than 75 years of growth that have established William Blair & Company as the leading private investment banking firm in the Midwest.

Today, William Blair & Company, L.L.C. is a global investment firm offering investment banking, asset management, equity research, and institutional and private brokerage to individual, institutional, and issuing clients. The firm still enjoys client relationships that began in the 1940s and has cultivated many other long-term partnerships by carrying on its philosophy of serving its clients' interests and objectives. Like its enduring relationships, this independent and employee-owned firm also places a high value on the quality of its products and services and the continuity and integrity of its people.

With its headquarters in Chicago, William Blair & Company operates 10 offices worldwide, including in Boston, London, New York, San Francisco, Shanghai, and Zurich. The firm has always supported the communities it serves and, since 1980, the William Blair & Company Foundation has continued to contribute to a broad range of causes—from youth-oriented educational activities to healthcare research. Building on the firm's tradition of providing excellent investment advice and advisory expertise in growth financing, William Blair & Company is helping shape the future of companies and communities around the world.

After Harry Kraemer's stirring keynote introduction to the New Leader's Centennial Summit, "Chicago's Got Talent: How to Have a Starring Role in Your Career," CDW's Catherine O'Connor facilitated a Q&A session with the energetic Northwestern University professor.

A COMMUNITY FOCUS WITH A GLOBAL OUTLOOK

The New Leader's Centennial Summit, held on November 2nd, was the fourth and final summit of The Club's Centennial Celebration. In truth, nearly every event on The Club's centennial year schedule shared the celebratory feel of its special summits. Among the four summits, however, none were more culturally dynamic and perhaps globally significant than the program that led off the second half of the year.

After its traditional break in July and August, The Club hosted the "U.S.–India Economic Opportunities and Synergies Summit" on September 20th, also at the Fairmont. Organized in partnership with the Federation of Indian Chambers of Commerce and Industry and in collaboration with The Chicago Council on Global Affairs and The Delhi Committee of Chicago Sister Cities, this one-day program featured presen tations and breakout sessions connecting governmental leaders of India with Chicago's business community. Like the international conferences of The Club's past, this event was aimed at fostering new business relationships between Chicago and the major cities of India.

With Rahm Emanuel quickly getting busy in the City Hall office that was for 22 years the domain of Richard M. Daley, it was no surprise he opened the event with welcoming words and a bold pledge. In fact, in briefly introducing the new mayor, Melissa Bean reminded the audience of the nickname her former congressional colleague earned in Washington to go with his reputation for getting things done, "Rahmbo."

Early in his remarks, Emanuel recalled President Barack Obama's relationship-building visit to India the previous year, and announced the first trade mission of his mayoral administration would be to India. He cited the promise

of business collaboration in the areas of manufacturing, aviation, pharmaceuticals and alternative energy, and expressed confidence that Indian companies will consider Chicago as a place to establish their U.S. headquarters.

Speaking after the mayor, both Harsh Mariwala, president of the Federation of Indian Chambers of Commerce and Industry and chairman of the India-based Marico Ltd., and His Excellency Anand Sharma, the country's Minister of Commerce, Industry and Textiles, also emphasized the rewarding prospects of mutual investment. Sharma highlighted a recently released report by Deloitte LLP that put India second, behind China, in the report's global manufacturing competitiveness index. "We are a nation of determined people," Sharma said. "We will go to double-digit growth in the years to follow." He also confirmed the next meeting of the India Business Forum (IBF) would be held in Chicago.

(Above) At The Club's U.S.–India Economic Opportunities and Synergies Summit on September 20th, Mayor Emanuel met with Anand Sharma, India's Minister of Commerce, Industry and Textiles, before the event got underway. (Above left) The Club's Melissa Bean greeted a number of distinguished guests throughout the daylong Summit.

The day continued with a series of panel discussions exploring industries where relationships between businesses in the two countries are yielding gains, and where more partnerships could prove profitable. In a morning session titled, "Opportunity in India," a question from the audience that referenced the Deloitte report and India's competitive comparison to China drew a quick-witted analogy from panelist R.V. Kanoria, Chairman and Managing Director of the India-based Kanoria Chemicals & Industries Limited. "The elephant moves more surely," he said. "It involves consensus, such as a democracy."

In its effort to feed the world's growing population, PotashCorp moves more than 30 million tons of material around the world each year.

POTASH

With operations and business interests in seven countries, Potash Corporation is an international enterprise at the frontlines of the immense challenge to feed the world's growing population. It is the world's largest fertilizer company by capacity, producing the three primary crop nutrients—potash, phosphate, and nitrogen. It is also the world's leading potash producer, making the corporation responsible for nearly 20 percent of global capacity.

Owned for many years by the Government of Saskatchewan, Potash Corporation unlocked its potential to impact global food production when it transitioned to an independent, publicly held organization in 1989. "Privatization allowed us to eradicate inefficiencies and reshape the environment and focus of the company," said William Doyle, President and Chief Executive Officer of Potash since 1999. "We were able to gain the positioning to be effective in the marketplace and take advantage of expansion opportunities."

An integral member of the company's senior management team during its turnaround, Doyle was among the leaders who guided acquisitions in the 1990s that strengthened its operations and capabilities. The team recognized—before it became apparent to the world—the importance of potash, phosphate and nitrogen products in providing the primary nutrients that crops need. "We could see where the market was going," said Doyle. This included the prospect of more global customers using these mineral products to make livestock feeds and industrial goods.

Acting on its agricultural projections, the company launched a bold strategy in 2003 to expand its global footprint while fortifying its relationships with customers closer to home. Though it remains a Canadian corporation, PotashCorp's commercial base in Northbrook, Illinois, has provided the company with a presence in the center of the Corn Belt—its largest market—and transportation accessibility to the breadbasket markets of North America and emerging markets around the world. "It's important to be close to our customer base, and to be able to move material by rail and people by air," said Doyle. "Chicago is a natural strategic location for us."

Contributing to and relying on Chicago's rise as a global business center, PotashCorp's reach now extends from China, the world's most populous nation and largest fertilizer consumer, and India, with its 1.2 billion people, to Latin America and the rice and oil palm producing fields of other Asian countries.

Technological advances have enhanced the company's ability to meet growing needs abroad and effectively respond to global market fluctuations. PotashCorp moves more than 30 million tons of material around the world each year through an international supply chain whose added efficiencies give it a 24/7 read on the marketplace.

Doing business with some developing countries, however, involves overcoming barriers of government corruption that includes leaders and groups that use food as a weapon to attain or retain power. "Governments can distort the marketplace and put up impediments, so we often have to go back and start again," said Doyle. "Of the world's nearly seven billion people, approximately one

billion are under nourished and a disproportion number of them are children, the most vulnerable members of society."

In new markets, reaching consumers takes time and continuity. Preparing a potash mine for operation can be a 10-year process. When it comes to harvesting crops, the need to maximize the efficiency of farmland has never been greater, which makes fertilizer such a vital tool to help stem the tide of time.

The amount of farmable land per person is diminishing. The world's population is rising. With that, there is an increasing demand for higher quality diets of fruits and vegetables and protein from crop-fed livestock. Every crop that's harvested removes nutrients from the soil, which must be replaced to keep soil healthy and productive. Fertilizers feed plants, which help to feed animals and people. In fact, fertilizer is responsible for more than 40 percent of the world's total crop yield. "Yet, over the next 40 years, the world will consume more food than has been consumed to this point," said Doyle. "The effort to increase yields to keep pace with population growth is a daunting challenge."

With a workforce that embraces the urgency of its obligation to help feed the world, PotashCorp has nurtured a culture that encourages leadership at every level. "It's a meritocracy, which means you get ahead in the company not by who you know, but what you know," said Doyle, a Chicago native. "Everyone here has the chance to become CEO, but our culture of teamwork and ingenuity is at the center of everything we do."

It is in providing young employees with opportunities to contribute to the success of a team that the company inspires and develops their distinct leadership skills. As an organization serving a global population, PotashCorp has made a priority of building a diverse team of employees. "Diversity and leadership development are paramount to our commitment to the next generation," said Doyle.

Along with investments in organizational infrastructure—including a $7.8 billion investment in its potash capability—the company contributes to the communities in which it operates through charitable contributions and employee volunteer efforts. From bringing its Coaching Kids on Crop Nutrients program to elementary schools in suburban Chicago to launching a $1 million matching gift challenge in support of Saskatchewan's food banks, PotashCorp strives to integrate agricultural education into its philanthropic initiatives.

After all, education and innovation are key elements to the global community's ability to prepare for the future. "Ultimately, working together, we have to find a way to feed 9.2 billion people," said Doyle. In his 38 years in the industry, Doyle hasn't always been optimistic about the task of multiplying food production to meet population growth projections. "But we have seen progress," he said. "In places like Africa, we have seen the quality of life improve virtually overnight in certain countries. If we continue to help people in their communities move from a dependence on food aid to agricultural self-reliance, then we can continue to make progress on one of the greatest challenges of our time."

MESIROW FINANCIAL

When Norman Mesirow purchased a seat on the New York Stock Exchange (NYSE) in 1937, he launched a one-man brokerage firm that would evolve into a leading Chicago-based financial services firm and one of the largest independent financial services firms in the Midwest. Today, Mesirow Financial is an employee-owned company with more than 1,200 employees serving the financial needs and goals of diverse clients through offices across the country and in London.

Since 1994, Mesirow Financial experienced an expansive growth period having made more than 50 acquisitions including KPMG LLP's U.S. Corporate Recovery practice in 2004, which established its Consulting Division. It was also the year that Mesirow Financial established its Currency Management department and named Diane Swonk chief economist of the firm.

Chairman and Chief Executive Officer Richard S. Price espouses the firm's core values of innovation, integrity, building long-term relationships and social responsibility. These attributes allow Mesirow Financial to better understand, anticipate and meet its clients' changing financial needs with a multitude of high-quality products and services. Its commitment to Chicago is practiced through active support of numerous organizations, many of which focus on children and their families. In addition, Mesirow Financial employees established a Going Green Committee to share, promote and apply innovative ideas that shape an eco-friendly impact within the organization.

Well capitalized and well positioned for the future, Mesirow Financial continues to leverage its leadership and expertise in the investment management, global markets, insurance and consulting sectors to achieve consistent, long-term results for individuals, institutions and organizations around the world.

Norman Mesirow launched a one-man brokerage firm that today is a leading Chicago-based financial services firm and one of the largest independent financial services firms in the Midwest.

Being greeted with nodding smiles, he then acknowledged the elephant in the room. "China doesn't have to get consensus to move."

Among the seven other sessions of the day was a conversation on aviation and infrastructure, moderated by Michael Wascom, Managing Director of International and Government Affairs for American Airlines, and another focusing on manufacturing, which was led by Tim Hanley, Global Manufacturing and Industry Leader at Deloitte LLP. A casual cocktail reception that included closing remarks by Melissa Bean and Harsh Mariwala brought the day to a close with the feeling that the world's oldest democracy and the world's largest democracy are poised to make great progress together in the years to come.

GUIDANCE THAT SUPPORTS CAREER DISCOVERIES

Just two days after The Club's U.S.-India Summit, many of its members took a field trip of sorts to the city's northern suburbs. The tranquil corporate headquarters of Discover Financial Services, in Riverwoods, served as the setting for a breakfast conversation with three of the region's most recognized chief executives on what it takes to climb to the executive position.

"Getting to the C-Suite," another event of the New Leaders Circle Leadership Development Program, welcomed guests to a comfortable café at Discover impressively framed by a wall-length window that looks out on a picturesque prairie. Tables positioned on three modest tiers peered down on a stage

Discover's David Nelms set a candid and casual tone at the New Leaders Circle Event, "Getting to the C-Suite."

tucked inside the café's curved glass wall.

CDW's Catherine O'Connor once again handled the introductions to the sell-out crowd. On this day she proudly introduced David Nelms, Chairman and CEO of Discover and Chairman of The Club's Board at this time, John Edwardson, Chairman of the Board of Directors of CDW, and Robert Parkinson, Chairman and CEO of Baxter.

With Nelms in many ways acting as host, he took to the microphone first and quickly set a relaxed and often humorously self-deprecating tone that would carry through to the program's lively question and answer session. Sharing anecdotes from his life and career—and threading insight and advice within each tale—he made the case that a career is, above all, a constant pursuit of learning.

The best lessons, Nelms contended, often come from taking risks and from experiencing failure. "Learn as much as you can at each step," he said. As Nelms went on to illustrate, the steps of a career don't typically follow pre-conceived notions. He talked about getting an internship at Johnson & Johnson and then choosing not to go into healthcare. He talked of having a chance to work for Disney but choosing instead to accept an offer in the insurance industry. "You learn things in parts of your career that you can apply to another career," he said.

Mentioning that one highlight of his early career at Discover was helping to establish the platinum card, Nelms also owned up to an error in his department that cost the company a significant amount of money. "I took responsibility," he said. "It was under my watch so I offered to resign." The company did not accept his resignation and, now, as the leader of Discover he is sensitive to work pressures but also insistent that professionals take ownership of each role they play. "Your happiness comes from how much you contribute and how much you learn," he advised the audience. "Work hard and remember to have fun."

Both echoing and expounding on the insight Nelms imparted, Robert Parkinson also rejected the idea that a career path can be engineered or mapped out in advance. "That's not how life really works," he said. After holding

RR DONNELLEY

When Richard Robert Donnelley founded the company that bears his name in 1864, a slender Illinois politician resided in the White House. With RR Donnelley's original Chicago printing facility growing strong in the age of Lincoln, the company was preparing to open a new operation in the city when the Great Chicago Fire broke out in 1871. Its new printing plant was destroyed, along with the home of its founder.

Without adequate insurance to rebuild the business, Donnelley asked his customers to write a recommendation for him on a piece of ledger paper. With this testament to his reputation for integrity, quality, and superb service as collateral, he traveled to New York and was able to borrow enough money to restart the business. By 1873, the building that had been destroyed by fire was rebuilt.

Today, the ledger paper from 1871 is displayed at RR Donnelley's headquarters in Chicago as a challenge to employees to continue building on the reputation of the company and its founder. That the company printed the original Burnham Plan for Chicago and the Centennial Edition a century later—as well as produced materials for the Columbian and Century of Progress Exhibitions—is evidence that RR Donnelley's employees have been responding to that challenge for generations.

As RR Donnelley's relationship with Chicago approaches 150 years—the company printed the original Burnham Plan for Chicago—it reflects on decades of growth that has led to an expansion of products and services currently reaching customers in approximately 40 countries across 14 different time zones.

As the company's relationship with Chicago approaches 150 years, its decades of growth has led to an expansion of products and services that now reach customers in approximately 40 countries across 14 different time zones.

While many still think of RR Donnelley as a printer, the company helps customers prepare, produce, deliver, and process integrated communications. Its base in the Chicago area encompasses several manufacturing facilities, substantial logistics operations, a full service Premedia operation, and other locations and its continuing stream of proprietary solutions includes high-speed color digital presses that RR Donnelley has designed, built, and deployed. These state-of-the-art presses are used in applications that include print-on-demand books, innovative documents that cross over between transactional and promotional messaging, and direct response materials that combine conventional and digitally produced content. The company has also introduced several mobile applications and offers a suite of Internet-based services for which more than 1.3 million business users have created profiles.

As President and Chief Executive Officer of what is now known as R. R. Donnelley & Sons Company, Thomas Quinlan III leads a global workforce of approximately 58,000 employees who have helped the company grow into the largest provider of printing and print-related business services in the world. "With annual revenues of more than $10.6 billion, and more than 600 locations around the globe, we continue to strengthen our services and products to meet the needs of our business customers wherever they may be," said Quinlan, who joined RR Donnelley in 2004 when the company acquired Moore Wallace. "Adding the resources of an established communications company like Moore Wallace has been a key aspect in the ongoing development of our broad offerings." Having previously served as Executive Vice President, Operations, at Moore Wallace, Quinlan's initial responsibilities at RR Donnelley included overseeing the integration of the two companies.

With RR Donnelley catering to the global business community, its brand may not be fully familiar to everyday consumers. Yet, on a daily basis, it's likely that most consumers see or interact with something the company had a hand in producing.

"We may have produced the retail insert from a newspaper that people take along with them to go shopping," said Quinlan. "In the store, they may see signage, product tags and labels, cash register receipts, and other materials that we produced. If they order online, there's a good chance that we produced the mailing label that directs their purchase to them as well as the promotional materials that are in the box along with the items they ordered."

Often working behind the scenes, RR Donnelley's preparation, production, and delivery processes center on helping its business customers increase the return on investment of their communications, meet compliance obligations, better communicate with their audiences, and accurately and efficiently complete transactions. From providing design services and digital asset management to printing books and magazines to warehousing and managing business process outsourcing, the company continues to carry on a Chicago tradition of service that now stretches around the world.

In one session of The Club's "Chicago's Got Talent" summit, Dave Thomas, Sales Director at PepsiCo, joined Philip Styrlund, CEO of the Summit Group, in a conversation on sales skills that lead to improved revenues.

a variety of leadership positions in his 25-year career at Abbott Laboratories, Parkinson was Dean of Loyola University Chicago School of Business Administration and Graduate School of Business before returning to the corporate sector as chairman and CEO of Baxter.

Rising to the c-suite of an organization, according to Parkinson, involves gaining experience in multiple areas of a company and accumulating knowledge about all aspects of a particular industry. He also warned that ambition, for some, can be a destructive quality. "Focus on the job you have, not the one you want," he said. "People will notice when you are not a team player. You have to have a passion and a love for what you do to really stand out."

Challenging the audience, Parkinson also said those who aspire to the c-suite should first answer why. "Know the answer to that question, because not everyone is interested in [that role]," he said. "And remember that your most important attribution is your reputation, your personal brand. You have to nurture it and protect it."

For his part, Edwardson took Parkinson's challenge a step further. "Many professionals want to be in the c-suite for all the wrong reasons," he said. He then related a story about one of his teenaged daughters accusing him of telling others what to do at work all day and then coming home to tell his children what to do. "I told her, 'I don't tell others what to do at work,'" Edwardson quipped with a smile. "She said, 'Then don't do it here.'"

Igniting laughter in the crowd, he went on to share stories and experiences about how he learned that true leadership isn't about being the sole decision-maker. Admitting he didn't have the best listening skills early in his career, he told the crowd about once being confronted by a mentor about his resolute mindedness. "He told me, 'If you stifle others by being right about everything, people won't want to work for you,'" Edwardson said. "It was one of the best conversations of my life."

Edwardson went on to hold leadership positions at Ameritech Corporation and United Airlines and was Chairman and CEO of Burns International Services Corporation before joining CDW in January 2001. "It's impossible to plan your way to the c-suite," Edwardson concluded. "Listening, learning, and hard work are by far the most important elements."

Like Nelms, Edwardson and Parkinson have served as chairman of The Executives' Club. Bringing them together in this way, in this setting, and on this subject was an opportunity for The Club to do something a little different, according to Melissa Bean. "We worked with David and others at Discover on this idea," she said. "With the change of scenery, we also adjusted the seating of guests to encourage further networking." Each corporate table at the event included one or two company representatives rather than a whole team. "This left other guests to fill in the table and meet and talk with leaders from a particular company," Bean said. "It seemed to work quite well."

AN EXCHANGE OF INSIGHT WITH RECOGNITION OF EXCELLENCE

In the time between this September event and its "Chicago's Got Talent" career summit at the start of November, The Club kept up its rhythm of programs with centennial flair that worked quite well. The Chicago CEO

BMO HARRIS BANK

In 1861, BMO Financial Group found its first Chicago home on South Water Street, opening its doors to the Chicago public as a customer and community focused bank. As a founding member of the Chicago Clearing House in 1865, BMO played a prominent role in the rebuilding of the city after the Great Chicago Fire of 1871, becoming a principal facilitator of the city's export trade.

Helping America expand westward, N.W. Harris also arrived in Chicago in the early 1880s. In the midst of the city's grand rebuilding effort, Harris formed N.W. Harris & Co. as an investment-banking firm. Supporting the financial needs and ventures of the local business community for the next 25 years, the firm became Harris Trust and Savings Bank in 1907 and expanded its customer base as well as its services. And in 1984, BMO Financial Group acquired Harris Bankcorp, Inc.

In 1847, Samuel Marshall rented half of a Milwaukee cobbler shop and opened Samuel Marshall & Co., Exchange Brokers. He was joined by Charles Ilsley two years later. Together, they built one of Wisconsin's premier financial institutions—Marshall & Ilsley Corporation—on the principles of quality and service. Like BMO, its customer philosophy was deeply rooted in service excellence and active community participation.

On July 5, 2011, the two companies were joined together as BMO Financial Group acquired Marshall & Ilsley Corporation. At this time, Harris N.A. changed its name to BMO Harris Bank N.A.

Today, with the rich, combined histories of Harris and M&I, BMO Harris Bank shares a strong commitment to customers and the community through its annual contribtion of financial support, investment capital, and in-kind contributions to community organizations. Its focus on financial literacy and community and economic development includes investing in areas to support affordable housing and small businesses, and its employees provide hundreds of volunteer hours to numerous organizations and causes. BMO Harris Bank received two 2010 Community Service Leadership Awards from Financial Services Roundtable based on the community efforts of Harris Bankcorp, Inc. and Marshall & Ilsley Corporation.

With a strong branch presence throughout Illinois, Indiana, Wisconsin, Minnesota, Missouri, Kansas, Florida and Arizona, BMO Harris Bank has been consistently recognized for the strength of its customer service.

In the 1890s, the Bank of Montreal Chicago Agency was located at 27 South LaSalle Street.

Breakfast in early October saw Jeff Smisek, President and CEO of United Continental Holdings, provide a leadership perspective on the ongoing integration of Continental and United Airlines and its future impact on Chicago. The Club's Technology Conference on October 26th at the Renaissance Blackstone Chicago Hotel featured a conversation with leaders of Mayor Emanuel's tech team on ways the new administration is working to improve the efficiency of government business and create an environment that supports innovative companies and ideas.

At the Technology Conference, The Club also presented Stewart McCutcheon, Chief Information Officer at Nalco, with the 2011 CIO of the Year award. The Executives' Club's CIO of the Year award, established in 2003, recognizes the increasingly important role CIOs play in value realization and the delivery of exceptional ROI, as well as the importance of technology in the Chicago economy McCutcheon was selected from a field of 27 top IT executives at some of the region's largest and best-known companies. "This is one way The Club seeks to facilitate knowledge transfer between CIOs and other senior executives," said Melissa Bean.

When the Technology Conference was ending its morning session at the Renaissance Blackstone, an audience was gathering at the Continental ABC room of The Hilton Chicago to hear Irene Rosenfeld, Chairman and CEO of Kraft Foods, address the Chicago economy and explore ways that companies like Kraft can weather the global recession. At this Global Leaders Luncheon, Rosenfeld made news by announcing she will stay on to lead one of the two publicly traded companies that Kraft plans to split into by the end of 2012. She also indicated that both companies would remain headquartered in the Chicago area.

By the end of October, Catherine O'Connor and the New Leaders Advisory Board had preparations in place for the "Chicago's Got Talent" summit, which included much more than Harry Kraemer's inspiring opening notes. The morning continued with a panel session on developing skills to meet market expectations and the ways that a presence on LinkedIn can help promote a personal brand and strengthen an organization's outreach. In the session, "Connecting to Revenue: Sales Skills for the Non-Sales Professional," moderator Coleen Byrne, an author and former Sales Director at Yahoo, drew compelling personal stories and powerful professional tips from Dave Thomas, Sales Director at PepsiCo, and Philip Styrlund, CEO of the Summit Group.

After an illuminating consultation by Maureen Costello, President of Image Launch, on simple and smart ways for professionals to enhance their personal appearance and visual image—complete with before and after photos—attendees of the summit celebrated the day and its valuable takeaways at a cocktail reception in the Fairmont's cabaret-style Moulin Rouge Ballroom.

Six days later, Mayor Emanuel would return to The Club. Like many of his predecessors, he would detail the plans and priorities of his administration and pledge his partnership with the organization and its members—extending a practice and a promise that, in The Club's centennial year, had long been a hallmark of its history.

1980—2000

RESPONDING TO CHALLENGES WITH UNIFIED RESOLVE

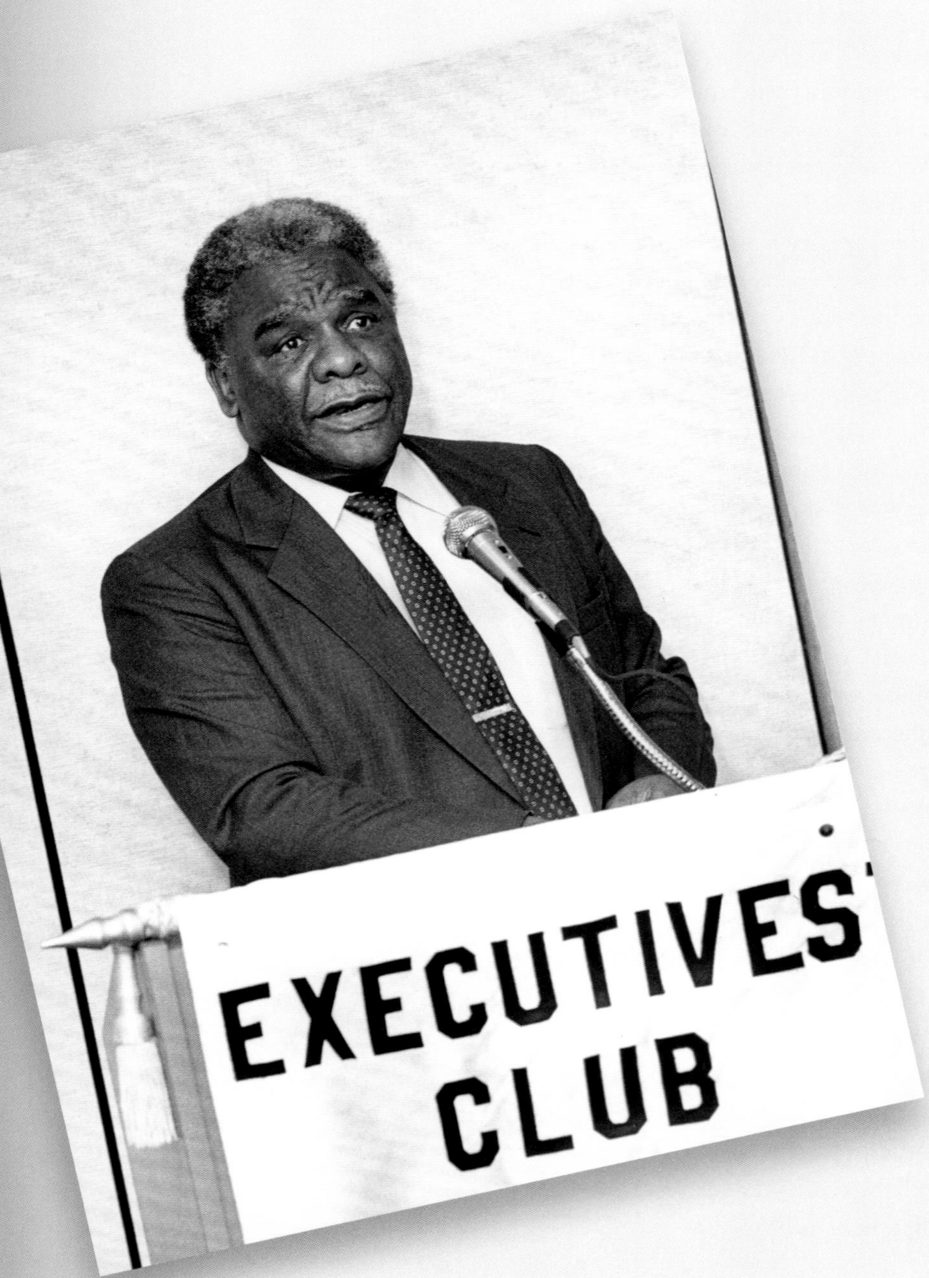

When Jane Byrne took over the mayor's office from Michael Bilandic in 1979, one of her first stops as the city's first female mayor was to The Executives' Club of Chicago. After all, The Club's long and harmonious relationship with Richard J. Daley had fortified its role in fostering cooperation between city government and the business community. A year after outlining her optimistic plans, the new mayor returned to The Club and delivered a State of the City address acknowledging the thorny challenges that come with the job and accentuating the importance of working together.

"What is Chicago?" Mayor Byrne posited to the lunch gathering on May 2, 1980. "It's a town that won't let you down, and it never has. It's got everything for the suburbanites, for world travelers, for conventioneers, for business. It's a great city...I'd like to see the cooperation of everybody in this room to help us make this city the greatest city in the world, an international gem; and I believe it can be done. But I believe it can be done only with your help."

That cooperative spirit endured but was tested in the economic sluggishness of the early 1980s. Mayor Byrne confronted issues with the local school board and a strike by the city's fire fighters among other challenges in her term. Despite the advent of another milestone for the city—the election of its first African American mayor in 1983—the "Council Wars" that greeted Mayor Harold Washington shortly after his swearing-in

Volume 56, No. 22 Chicago, Illinois 60602 April 25, 1980

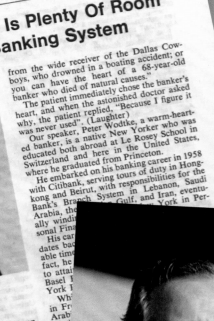

Swiss Banker: There Is Plenty Of Room For All In U.S. Banking System

Peter G. Wodtke
Executive Vice President,
Swiss Bank Corporation

PRESIDENT WHITE: Good afternoon, ladies and gentlemen. My name is Bill White. As President of The Executives' Club I am delighted to welcome you to luncheon here today.

Long famous for their artistry in the handling of other people's money, the Swiss enjoy an impeccable reputation for shrewdness, honesty, and secrecy in matters of finance. There are as many stories of numbered accounts and couriers carrying fortunes in briefcases as there are mystery writers, but I doubt if very many of us are aware of the international scope of organizations such as the Swiss Bank Corporation.

We have as our guest speaker today an

from the wide receiver of the Dallas Cowboys, who drowned in a boating accident; or you can have the heart of a 68-year-old banker who died of natural causes."

The patient immediately chose the banker's heart, and when the astonished doctor asked why, the patient replied, "Because I figure it was never used". (Laughter)

Our speaker, Peter Wodtke, a warm-hearted banker, is a native New Yorker who was educated both abroad at Le Rosey School in Switzerland and here in the United States, where he graduated from Princeton.

He embarked on his banking career in 1958 with Citibank, serving tours of duty in Hongkong and Beirut, with responsibilities for the Bank's Branch System in Lebanon, Saudi Arabia, the Gulf, and Iran, eventually windi York in Personal Fina

ceremony kept the city's government leaders locked in a struggle for power until 1986.

In the midst of his ongoing tug-of-war with a majority bloc of alderman, Mayor Washington sought an audience with The Club to make his case for the city's need to enact his policies of reform. His address to The Club, on March 30, 1984, was the first of a series of reform-focused speeches delivered throughout the city in the weeks that followed.

"I am convinced, after ten or eleven months, that the mayor of Chicago must have the energy of a distance runner and lungs of an ox, and some other attributes which I will not mention," the mayor quipped at the outset of his remarks. "Suffice it to say, it has been a very hectic ten months, a very rewarding ten months, and I hope ten months which have just at least indicated in which direction in general we wish to head this vast ship of city called Chicago."

Washington gained a mantle of influence over the next two years and was reelected in 1987. But just a few months after his appearance in March of 1984, The Executives' Club was working to keep the tide of its own momentum from screeching to a halt. After seven decades of service to the city and its business interests, The Club was in danger of shutting its doors.

In May of 1984, The Club elected new members to its Board of Directors. Diane Mayne, a partner at the Chicago law firm Seyfarth, Shaw, Fairweather & Geraldson was elected Chairman. That she was the first female to hold this position at The Club would have been enough to make her Chairmanship stand out in the organization's long history. That she was among an instrumental few who helped the organization overcome profound difficulties makes her term in this leadership post all the more memorable.

Mayne had come to Chicago in the late 1960s with a Masters Degree in Social Work. She landed a job with the state and found herself working alongside attorneys crafting contracts between state government and private agencies. Recognizing limited growth opportunities for women in most any field at that time, she developed an interest in law and was accepted to the DePaul University College of Law. She attended classes in the evening and, after graduating, started a career practicing corporate law at Seyfarth, Shaw, Fairweather & Geraldson.

When Mayne first interviewed with the firm, she already knew they had female attorneys on staff. She was convinced that

TENNECO

Emerging as a standalone company in 1999, Tenneco has become a global leader in developing the latest automotive technologies and products for customers around the world. Headquartered in Lake Forest, Illinois, the company operates nearly 80 manufacturing facilities and 14 engineering centers located in 24 countries.

It is Tenneco's combination of leading-edge technology, manufacturing expertise, and dedication to customer service that has spurred its growth as one of the world's leading designers, manufacturers and distributors of emission control and ride control products and systems for the automotive original equipment market and the aftermarket. With well-balanced product lines and globally-recognized brands, Tenneco's 22,000 employees worldwide share a culture of teamwork, integrity, and continuous improvement. Dedicated to manufacturing products that clean the environment and improve driver comfort and safety, Tenneco's environmental stewardship extends to the health and safety of its employees, customers, and communities.

In delivering the best quality, performance and service found in its industry, Tenneco has increased revenues to $5.9 billion annually and is well positioned to capture significant revenue growth as stricter light and commercial vehicle emission regulations are implemented in many worldwide markets. Behind the strength and skill of its global team of employees, the company will continue to build on its reputation as a pioneer in global ideas for cleaner, quieter, smoother, and safer transportation.

becoming a partner was a possibility. Once she joined the ranks of partner, Mayne explored outside opportunities to enhance her view of the business world. In the early '80s she was attracted to The Executives' Club after learning their speakers included Terry Savage and other female business leaders. She joined and was quickly invited to participate in one of its committees.

The Club at that time still centered on a set speaker's forum, held each Friday during the lunch hour. Through the luncheons and her committee work, Mayne met business-men and women of many industries and got to know other lawyers in the city. Helen Thatcher, then the Associate Dean of The John Marshall Law School, was among the members she counted as a friend.

"Every Friday all of these people got together and we had a lovely lunch, a presentation, and a reception," said Mayne, who is now enjoying her retirement in New Mexico and goes by her married name, Diane Mueller. "It was impressive and everything seemed to be running very smoothly."

When Mayne was elected chairman, she was excited to learn Thatcher was elected secretary of The Club. Both women were aware that membership in The Club was on the decline amid the economic downturn of the early '80s. But it wasn't long before the two of them and other Board members noticed signs of deeper organizational problems.

"We began to see that the financial picture was not very good," said Mayne. They also learned that staff members of The Club had not lined up a full roster of speakers far enough in advance—typically, the staff would be working six months ahead of the

Executives' Club News

Page 12

Verne B. Leedy
Chairman

James L. Oleson
First Vice Chairman

Chester A. Warner
Secretary

ELECTION OF OFFICERS AND DIRECTORS

At the 69th Annual Meeting of The Executives' Club of Chicago, the
Directors were elected by the members.

OFFICERS

For Chairman
Verne B. Leedy
Assistant to Division Superintendent -
Steel Products
U.S. Steel Corporation

For Secretary
Chester A. Warner
Principal Associate
Corporate Growth Development Associates

For First Vice Chairman
James L. Oleson
Senior Account Executive
Merrill Lynch

DIRECTORS FOR TWO YEAR

*Victor A. Anderson
Insurance Broker
Corroon & Black of Illinois, Inc.
*John T. Boyd
President
Right Girl Temporary Service, Inc.
*Lester W. Brann, Jr.
President
Illinois State Chamber of Commerce
**Michael E. Breslin
Senior Vice President - General
Counsel
Leo Burnett, Inc.
**C. Chester Carlson
President
C. C. Carlson Company
*Charles A. Comiskey II
Investments
**Gertrude D. Crain
Chairman of the Board
Crain Communications, Inc.
*Henry A. Dembosz
President & General Manager
Zenith Distributing Corporation of Illinois
**V. Peter Ferrara
President
Nelson-Hall Book Publishing Company
*Albert S. George
President
J. M. Bundscho, Inc.
**George B. Guthrie
Attorney at Law
* 1979-1981

schedule. With a budget in the red, a shrinking membership roll, and dates in the weekly speaker's schedule that would go unfilled, the Board let staff members go and took over supervisory control of the day-to-day operations.

The necessity of this move prompted a few business leaders associated with The Club to suggest, according to Mayne, that the organization might have outlived its usefulness. Mayne dismissed any notions of allowing the organization to fade away. "I knew there was a place for a civic organization that brought business leaders together," she said. "To me, a big city has to have something like that. There were just too many good, solid businesses in Chicago, and law firms, accounting firms, and people who would benefit from interacting with each other and keeping up with what was happening generally in the business world beside in their own individual businesses. And most of the CEOs that I knew at the time felt the same way."

This moral support was indeed important, but any effective turnaround strategy would have to be guided by a point person able to dedicate the necessary time and energy—and relieve the Board of day-to-day involvement. While carrying on with their own work obligations, Mayne and Thatcher began searching for a professional qualified to lead The Club's operations and restore management stability. "We were looking for more than a replacement. We were looking for someone to really revitalize The Club," said Mayne. "It was Helen who found Kaarina."

In 1985, Kaarina Koskenalusta was executive director of the Chicago-based Mid-America Committee, an organization dedicated to promoting public/private partnerships and serving as a forum to explore international economic policy and trade and investment issues. She had come to Chicago years earlier from her native Finland to study international politics.

Though happy in her career at Mid-America, Koskenalusta was intrigued by the call she received from Mayne concerning The Club's critical need to fill a leadership vacuum at the organizational level. "I was very excited about [our conversation] because it was a venerable organization and I thought that maybe we had an opportunity to revive it," recalled Kosken-alusta in an August 2010 interview.

In a follow-up meeting with Mayne and Thatcher, Koskenalusta learned more about the organization and the extent of its challenges. Their dialogue continued over the course of a few days before Mayne extended an offer. "We pulled no punches," said Mayne. "She was focused. I knew she had an international background. I knew she knew what she was doing. I knew she had perseverance…and I knew she would come to grips with problems."

In accepting the offer, Koskenalusta became The Club's first female President and CEO and was a force and fixture at The Club for the next 25 years. Her first days on the job, however, were spent organizing office documents and determining the status of upcoming events. According to Koskenalusta, there were two luncheons on the schedule but no sign of attendee registration information for them. "We started pretty much from the bottom up," she said.

Yet, The Club still had its reputation as a distinguished business forum. The platform it provided to notable industry leaders, entertainers, politicians, and professors over its 74 years had made its name recognizable and respected beyond the city it represented. As Mayne recalled, The Club leveraged the strength of its image and culled enough resources early in 1985 to set up a speaking engagement featuring former U.S. Secretary of State Alexander Haig. "I breathed a sigh of relief when I saw the turnout for that meeting because I thought, we're going to make it," said Mayne.

Business leaders began stepping up to lend support in a variety of ways, spurring on The Club's gradual shift in momentum. One executive offered budgetary guidance and others encouraged colleagues to join The Club or renew a membership. Real estate magnate Arthur Rubloff, a well-known figure in the city and a member of The Club, sent out personal invitations to peers and colleagues who might be interested in joining. Frank Considine, then CEO of American National Can Company, offered strategic guidance to The Club and also made a personal pitch on behalf of the organization. "Frank basically sent, on his CEO letterhead, a two sentence letter to business leaders saying, 'Please see to it that you take a membership in The Executives' Club,'" recalled Koskenalusta. "So, that was my introduction to how the CEOs work. It was and still is a tight knit community."

By the time Diane Mayne's term as chairman ended, in the spring of '85, executives and others responded to The Club's outreach and the effort to stabilize its membership gained ground. This opened the door to adding more CEOs to its Board, which was also in need of stability. In time, an Advisory Board of specialized professionals was also formed to provide The Club with more visionary insight and counsel. The organization's committees were gradually reshaped as well.

The new Board worked with Koskenalusta to revamp its programming schedule, moving from a format of weekly Friday luncheons to ten speaking events a year. Ultimately becoming

JONES LANG LASALLE

With more than 40,000 professionals working across 1,000 locations in 60 countries, Jones Lang LaSalle is a financial and professional services firm serving the local, regional and global real estate needs of its broad-based clients. Headquartered in Chicago and specializing in both real estate services and investment management, the company assembles teams of experts who deliver integrated services built on market insight and foresight, sound research, and relevant market knowledge.

Remarkably, the company's heritage is tied to 1783, when Richard Winstanley set up shop as an auctioneer in London. Through a series of partnerships, the Winstanley firm became known by the last names of its three principal members, Jones Lang Wootton (JLW) & Sons, in 1939. JLW began its global expansion in 1957 by opening offices in Australia and, later, New Zealand, Singapore, Kuala Lumpur, Hong Kong, and Tokyo.

By 1968, a small group of professionals leading a similar company outgrowing its base in Texas moved to Chicago, changed its name to LaSalle Partners, and blossomed into one of America's leading real estate service firms. JLW's opening of its first U.S. office in New York in 1975 set the stage for the eventual merger of JLW and LaSalle Partners in 1999. The largest international real estate industry merger to date formed a company that remains the leading global commercial real estate services and investment management firm.

Led by Colin Dyer, President and Chief Executive Officer, the award-winning company remains determined to be a good corporate citizen in every corner of its global community and to continually challenge its diverse and talented workforce to develop enduring client relationships built on quality service, integrity, collaboration, and trust.

In recent years Jones Lang LaSalle has continued to grow stronger through organic growth and strategic acquisitions that have increased its presence in key real estate and capital markets throughout the world.

the Global Leaders Luncheon Series, the focus was on presenting Fortune 100 CEOs.

By 1989, with speakers that included Vice President George Bush and Senator Robert Dole, it was again drawing big names and capacity crowds. Forging further interaction with senior governmental figures, The Club organized special briefings that brought leading members of The Club to the nation's capital to meet with administration officials and congressional representatives.

Having overcome a stretch of troublesome times, The Club boldly entered the 1990s with a mission to become "the premier business forum in America." In an increasingly competitive business environment, with Frank Considine serving a stint as chairman, that meant examining opportunities to take another step forward. Koskenalusta's international perspective and the success of The Club's briefings in Washington, D.C. inspired a series of organizational trips abroad. Delegations of members traveled to countries that included China, Russia, Belgium, the Czech Republic, Finland, France, Germany, Hungary, and Poland. At each destination, members met with senior government officials and business leaders to create strategic alliances and business partnerships.

This form of international relationship building aligned with the promotional philosophy of the city's new mayor. Richard M. Daley, elected in 1989, made an early commitment to not only working to retain the companies based in Chicago, but also to attracting other corporations to the city. Like his father, this mayor viewed The Executives' Club as an important instrument of civic leadership that represented Chicago's best interests close to home and around the world.

As the rise of the Internet and other advanced technologies continued to draw the world together, The Club honored Microsoft's Bill Gates with its first International Executive of the Year Award in 1995.

It was software pioneers like Gates that business leaders throughout the country wanted to learn from and perhaps emulate at the dawn of an increasingly global economy. The Club was able to land these headliners. On September 23, 1998, Eckhard Pfeiffer, then President and CEO of Compaq Computer Corporation, opened The Club's 1998-1999 CEO Luncheon Series, at the Palmer House Hilton. Michael Dell, Chairman and CEO of Dell Computer Corporation, took to the Palmer House podium a month later. To complement these types of presentations, The Club put together high-tech seminars and conferences.

The Club also added more international meetings, which included hosting a matchmaking conference with business leaders of the European Union. Whenever an international dignitary such as Lech Walesa, the President of Poland, or the president of the Republic of Hungary were to be welcomed at The Club, Mayor Daley enthusiastically agreed to take part in the event.

While adapting its programming to reflect the changing economic landscape,

The Club never abandoned its priority of strengthening relationships within the Chicago business community. It introduced newly arrived executives and companies to other corporate and civic leaders, and continued to blend local and regional corporate leaders into its schedule of speakers.

In December of 1998, Verne Istock, then President and CEO of First Chicago NBD Corporation and John McCoy, then Chairman & CEO Banc One Corporation, teamed up in a special holiday luncheon presentation. Jack Greenberg, then President and CEO of McDonald's Corporation spoke in March of 1999, and Donald Fites, then Chairman and CEO of Caterpillar Inc., addressed The Club in April of that year. In fact, The Club soon bolstered its support of locally based corporations by launching a Chicago CEO Breakfast Series specifically dedicated to exploring strategies to better compete in the global marketplace.

When Richard C. Notebaert, then Chairman of the Board of Ameritech, and Edward E. Whitacre Jr., then Chairman of the Board and Chief Executive Officer of SBC Communications Inc., presided at the special holiday luncheon of 1999, there was much to celebrate. The Club had capped another decade of service to a business community of ingenuity and a city of resilience. On the cusp of a new century—sure to be one of increasing complexity as well as remarkable progress—the organization exemplified its long held ideal that coming together is the only way to truly move forward.

For Melissa Bean, there couldn't have been a more exciting time to join the leadership of The Executives' Club than in its centennial year.

CHAPTER FIVE

DETERMINED TO BUILD ON A CENTURY OF SUCCESS

Coffee. Conversation. Hugs and handshakes. The swift exchange of business cards. The pre-game ritual of another Executives' Club event is underway in the spacious foyer of the Imperial Ballroom. It's this custom of connecting—with each gathering stirring a distinctive energy—that gives every event of The Club its own personality. As the sea of guests move from the foyer to their tables inside the ballroom on this chilly December morning, the feeling on the ground floor of the Fairmont Chicago is festive. After all, it's The Executives' Club of Chicago's final event of its Centennial Celebration.

What better way to wrap up this yearlong anniversary party of programming than with a Chicago CEO Breakfast? At each table in the packed ballroom, the harmony of laughter and good cheer seasons the meal, and the infectious vibe carries into a main course titled, "Leadership, Chicago-Style: Executive Insights on Competitiveness and Change."

Seated on stage with three other standout Chicago business leaders, Christie Hefner quickly and cleverly establishes her role as this morning's moderator. In introducing Brad Keywell, Co-founder and Director of Groupon, Inc., Ilene Gordon, Chairman and CEO of Corn Products International, and Patrick Ryan, CEO of Ryan Specialty Group LLC and founder and former chairman of Aon Corporation, Hefner categorizes the multigenerational panel of leaders as young, seasoned, and iconic. "These are the stages of my life, so I'm here as well," says the smiling former CEO of Playboy Enterprises, who is now Executive Chairman of Canyon Ranch Enterprises. The chuckling audience is, in fact, a collective mix of the life stages Hefner and her fellow panelists represent.

When The Executives' Club of Chicago initiated its corporate membership options in the late 1990s, the organization essentially flung open its doors to every tier of the Chicago business community. The newly minted corporate members not only began bringing groups of employees to The Club's events, they more frequently invited clients of various business levels to join them. Even before the formation of the New Leaders Circle, program seating that had historically been dominated by the executive class became consistently

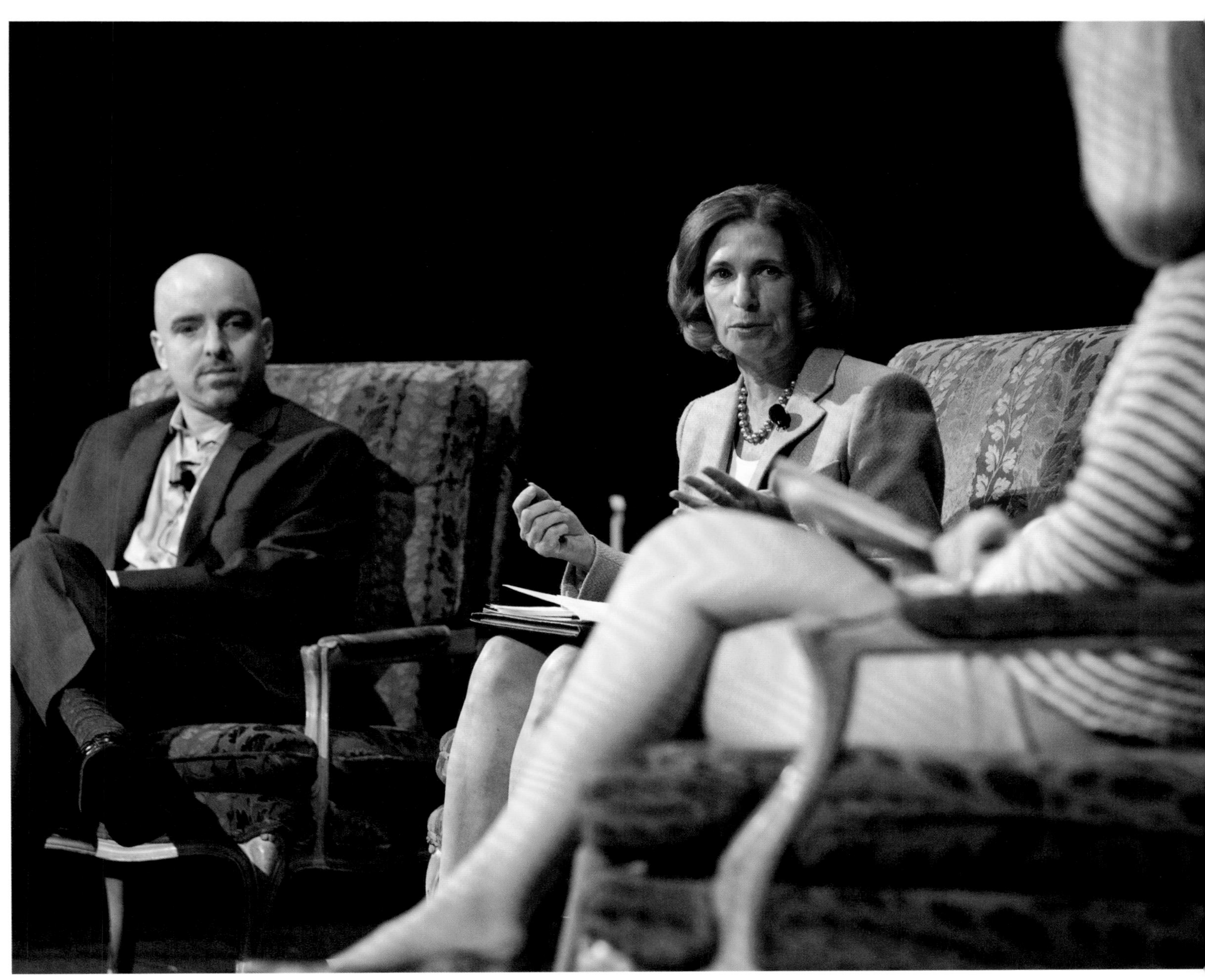

At the Chicago CEO Breakfast, "Leadership, Chicago-Style: Executive Insights on Competitiveness and Change," Brad Keywell and Ilene Gordon joined Pat Ryan in a wide-ranging discussion moderated by Christie Hefner.

Mayor Rahm Emanuel visited with David Nelms and Melissa Bean before his November 8th address at The Club titled, "The Future of Economic Development in Chicago."

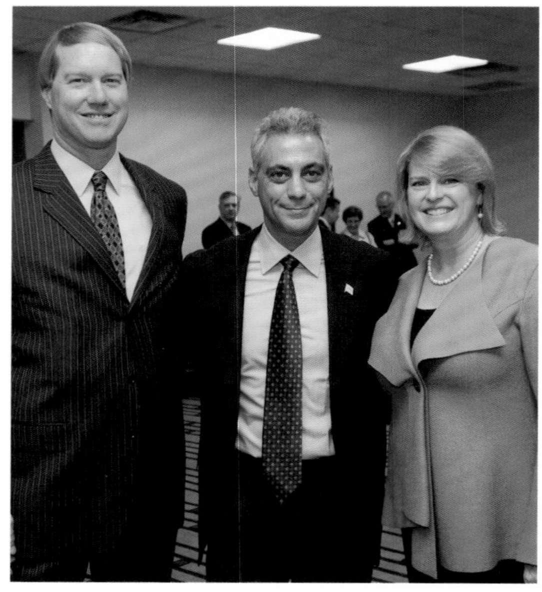

balanced with business development professionals, middle mangers, sales representatives, rising stars, and even prospective company recruits.

This broad inclusiveness stood out to Vish Rathnasabapathy when, in The Club's anniversary year, he began exploring organizations that could offer him opportunities to expand his business knowledge and his networking base. "I knew The Executives' Club presented some amazing business speakers, but I was actually surprised to learn how many different types of professionals you can connect with here," he says, just before Hefner opens the season's final Chicago CEO Breakfast.

An Executive Scholar of Northwestern University's Kellogg School of Management, Rathnasabapathy is Vice President of Strategy and Implementation at ACS Recovery Services, a Xerox Company. His membership in The Club is actually being processed as he hands his business card to those seated around him at the December 6th event. "I'm excited about all that I can gain from being a member," Rathnasabapathy says. "What I look forward to the most is the chance to meet new and interesting people, and to be part of a community that is dedicated to building on the incredible history of Chicago."

CONVERSATIONS THAT ALWAYS CONSIDER THE FUTURE

When the Chicago CEO Breakfast panel discussion drew to a close, the mingling continued. While many headed toward the ballroom's doors at the back of the room, Rathnasabapathy worked his way toward the stage to introduce himself to The Executives' Club's Melissa Bean. Other guests of the morning dialogue chatted with Hefner, Brad Keywell, Ilene Gordon, and Pat Ryan.

"When you look back on the history of this club, it's always been a place for business people to gather and share perspectives," Ryan said while shaking hands after the event. "To be here today as part of a multi-generational meeting shows how its commitment to that principle continues. The young people who are a part of this organization don't come to be seen. They are here to listen, to learn, and to contribute

Headquartered in the Chicago suburb of Vernon Hills, CDW has built a workforce of more than 6,400 and operations in 14 states and the District of Columbia.

CDW CORPORATION

For a number of years, Michael Krasny explored several different business opportunities without success. In 1982, as a 28-year-old in need of cash, he decided to place an ad to sell his own personal computer. The sale that came from the three-line, $3 classified ad for his used IBM actually amplified his fascination with computers and new technology. Recognizing the explosive growth potential for the computing industry, Krasny set out to capitalize on it by founding CDW in 1984. Quickly charting a distinct path, the fledgling company was among the first to market and sell computers directly to customers.

With a focus on selling a variety of computer products and building a corporate culture appealing to customers and coworkers alike, Krasny planted the seeds of CDW's evolution into a leading provider of technology solutions for business, government, education, and healthcare.

"Michael established an entrepreneurial spirit and a people-first culture that continues to inspire our young and energetic team of coworkers," said John A. Edwardson, Chairman and Chief Executive Officer of CDW since 2001. With broad business leadership experience that includes serving as president and, later, chief operating officer of UAL Corporation and United Airlines, Edwardson was brought on board to guide CDW's transition from a home-based Chicago area business to a Fortune 500 company with operations in 14 states and the District of Columbia. "When I joined CDW, my objective was to add to our infrastructure in a way that would help us grow without compromising the independence and innovation that shaped our early success," he said.

Now generating nearly $9 billion in annual revenue, CDW is ranked No. 38 on Forbes' list of America's Largest Private Companies. Its continued growth is driven by dedicated account managers helping customers choose the right technology products and services to best meet their needs, solution architects offering expertise in designing customized solutions, and advanced technology engineers assisting customers with the implementation and long-term management of those solutions. Its product offerings range from discrete hardware and software products to complex technology solutions that include data center optimization and cloud computing.

Headquartered in the Chicago suburb of Vernon Hills, with an office in downtown Chicago as well, CDW's longstanding commitment to corporate citizenship extends to the communities it serves around the country and beyond. With a workforce of more than 6,400, CDW coworkers have dedicated thousands of volunteer hours and the company has built partnerships and provided funding support to a variety of charitable causes and organizations. The company and its coworkers also responded—with fundraisers, technical support, and in some cases employee teams on the ground—to the 2004 tsunami off the coast of Indonesia, Hurricane Katrina in 2005, and the 2010 earthquake in Haiti.

"We've had special opportunities to be of help, whether providing technical assistance that improves communications capabilities in a crisis or, as in Hurricane Katrina, sending groups of employees to help rebuild homes and businesses," said Edwardson, who was part of one group that made the trip. "In our community efforts and our everyday work with customers, it's all about making things happen and getting things done. In building on our history of innovative solutions and our ability to adapt to new technologies and markets, we're excited to lead our company and our industry into the future."

Far right: George Ketchum (left), founder of Ketchum Publicity, talks with Walter Cronkite in 1952. Since its founding in Pittsburgh in 1923, Ketchum has grown to more than 2,000 employees operating in more than 70 countries with 100 offices and affiliates worldwide.

Right: Adm. Mike Mullen, Chairman of the Joint Chiefs of Staff, addresses global media in Chicago during a press conference arranged by Ketchum following his address to The Executives' Club of Chicago in August 2010.

KETCHUM

One of the largest and most recognized global public relations agencies, Ketchum characterizes its promise to clients around the world with two simple words; "break through." Cultivating bold, creative and unexpected ideas, the agency's command of communications helps clients across a range of industries stand out in the crowd. Its award-winning work builds brands, fortifies reputations, and produces results.

"I like to think of Ketchum not so much as a physical place, but as an idea," said Rob Flaherty, Senior Partner and President of Ketchum. "And the idea is that anything is possible if you can break through."

Fueling this spirit of possibility is the agency's five global practices—Brand Marketing, Corporate, Healthcare, Food & Nutrition, Technology—and a number of specialty areas that drive its public relations, marketing, and communications strategies in more than 65 countries. The bounty of accolades the agency has earned over its lifetime illustrates the depth of its dedication to all aspects of its work. Ketchum has won more Silver Anvils, the industry's highest honor, than any other agency.

While known for its creativity and enduring client relationships, the distinctive research Ketchum applies to all phases of the public relations process is also instrumental to its success. Through its Ketchum Global Research & Analytics network, investigative elements that range from planning and program development to tracking and outcome measurement contribute to communications campaigns that make a lasting impact. "The early research initiatives we developed to gain insight and information have served us well as new technologies have continued to alter the landscape of communications," said Flaherty, who joined Ketchum in 1989 and now works closely with CEO Ray Kotcher and other leaders to guide its performance.

Establishing Ketchum Digital five years ago is just one way the agency has enhanced its capacity to serve clients in a marketing age that demands analytical expertise as well as break through creativity. "Technology has raised the bar," said Flaherty. "There is no longer always a gatekeeper for content that reaches consumers. With this freedom, though, only smart and inventive strategies rise above the clutter."

In leading rather than following the industry trends of a new era, Ketchum carries on a tradition of ideas and innovation that dates back to the earliest days of public relations. In 1923, George Ketchum founded Ketchum Publicity to serve the advertising, fundraising, and publicity needs of local clients. A year later, the firm added the names of its partners to become Ketchum, MacLeod & Grove, or KM&G. By the 1940s, its steadily growing client list included Westinghouse Electric Company. Delivering skillful communications services, KM&G helped Westinghouse deal with a union strike.

From its valuable early experiences, the firm gained client assignments in the areas of product promotion and sales meeting programs. Working with Heinz, KM&G built a major publicity campaign that engaged consumers in donating millions of cans of baby food to children in Europe. In 1956, after landing advertising and public relations contracts with New York-based American Gas Association and Westinghouse Broadcasting Corporation, KM&G opened an office in New York. By the end of the 1960s, it had grown into one of the country's largest integrated public relations companies.

Positioning for another wave of growth and expansion in the 1980s, the agency's public relations business began operating as Ketchum Public Relations and in 1982 the company moved its headquarters to New York. Ketchum launched Camp Ketchum and Ketchum University in 1986. These staff-development programs were a first in the

industry and, along with the Ketchum Leadership Institute, continue to serve as employee training programs.

"Our strong values, integrity and spirit of collegiality are spurred by our Midwestern roots," said Flaherty. "That collective culture fosters our dedication to the success of our clients and our ongoing investment in our people." No matter the changes in the industry, Ketchum has always emphasized that successful relationships are personal. "In our business, you don't call an office," said Flaherty. "You call a person."

With relationships among its advantages in the 1990s, Ketchum secured one of its first global accounts, with Federal Express, and its first pan-European account, with Whirlpool. In 1995, it introduced industry-focused practices that included Food and Nutrition, Brand Marketing, Corporate, Technology, and Healthcare. Ketchum was twice named Agency of the Year by Inside PR in this decade, and its services and resources were strengthened when the agency was acquired by Omnicom Group in 1996.

In launching its global intranet portal in 2000, another innovation that gained industry recognition, Ketchum reinforced the cohesion of its employees around the world and introduced the Ketchum Programming Process, a disciplined six-step approach to handling client assignments. Leveraging its modern communications infrastructure, Ketchum combined its operations with Pleon, Europe's largest strategic communications consultancy, in 2009. Over the years, Ketchum has opened other offices abroad, including in India and China, making it one of the most geographically diverse public relations agencies in the world.

Today, with over 100 offices and affiliates, the company's office network allow team leaders in various outposts to conduct brainstorming sessions online. Ketchum has even designed a digital platform that engages students of participating universities. Inviting them to contribute fresh ideas to existing projects, the students earn experience and can also earn points to gain further mentoring and career advice. With a global perspective and a community focus, Ketchum's affiliates reflect the synergy of the business cultures in which they operate.

For years, Ketchum Midwest, comprised of Chicago and Pittsburgh, has advanced the company's public relations management of clients in the corporate communications, brand, and food and nutrition sectors and the team's work extends to community-building projects and pro bono services to nonprofit organizations. "Ketchum Midwest is central to our DNA as a company that drives brand results," said Flaherty.

Chicago is also home to one of Ketchum's fastest growing businesses. Created in 2007, Zócalo Group specializes in word-of-mouth marketing and is one of the first agencies of its kind. It is another example of Ketchum's determination to open productive channels of communication. "We're always learning, and always looking for new ways to give voice to our clients," said Flaherty. For nearly 90 years, Ketchum has charted a successful path by developing the skills and talent of its people, recognizing the needs and aspirations of its clients, and remaining true to its commitment to break through.

AMSTED

Amsted Industries is a leading supplier to the rail, vehicular and construction and building markets. Its products are manufactured by over 10,000 employees in plants throughout North America, Europe, Asia and South America, and are sold under well-established brand names, including Amsted Rail, Griffin Wheel, Brenco, ASF-Keystone, Consolidated Metco, Baltimore Aircoil, Griffin Pipe, Means, Burgess-Norton and Diamond Chain.

Many of the base technologies employed by Amsted's businesses—casting, forging and machining—date back to before its founding in 1902. Today Amsted employs these and other technologies in conjunction with advanced engineering and lean operations to produce innovative high-quality products at low cost. Together with an emphasis on customer intimacy and commercial discipline, this has led to leading market positions for virtually all of its products.

Since 1986, Amsted has been privately owned by its employee stock ownership plan (ESOP), becoming a wholly-owned S corporation ESOP in 1998. This structure gives employees "skin in the game," and has enabled Amsted to concurrently invest in its businesses for growth, while at the same time providing excellent retirement savings for its employees. The S-ESOP structure imposes disciplines that emphasize cash flow and high investment hurdles.

Over the last 10 years, under Chairman, President and Chief Executive Officer Bob Reum, Amsted has required its businesses to develop well-honed growth strategies that are subject to continuous internal challenge. In most cases these strategies have included expansion into global markets, where Amsted's businesses bring superior technologies. Key to achieving Amsted's continued success and growth will be the development of its people. The tremendous opportunities available to Amsted will require talent throughout the globe, and increasingly the company is focused on building that strength.

to its future. That's what is so impressive about The Executives' Club of Chicago."

The founder of a Chicago company that would become Aon Corporation, the world's largest global insurance broker, Ryan has, of course, been one of the city's most respected business leaders for the last four decades. He is just as recognized and admired for his civic deeds and devotion over the years. Days after the announcement in October of 2009 that Chicago had come up short in its bid to host the 2016 Olympics, Ryan reflected on the effort and its outcome at The Executives' Club.

The CEO of "Chicago 2016," as the city's bid committee was known, Ryan expressed disappointment but focused on the upsides. "Chicago has taken its rightful place as a global city," he told The Club's audience. Mayor Daley, who joined Ryan at the October 9, 2009 meeting, praised Ryan's leadership and reiterated the civic value of bringing people together in the process. "If you don't try, you fail," said Daley. "We will take this energy and use it for other purposes, such as our schools, crime or economic development."

Like his father, Daley often turned to The Executives' Club and leaders like Ryan to galvanize support for civic projects. The planning and development of Millennium Park in the early 2000s is just one high profile example.

At the Chicago CEO Breakfast in December, Ryan insisted the communal energy of the Olympic bid is still very much alive. The influence and accomplishments of the panelists sitting next to him perhaps best illustrated this point.

It's well known that Hefner extended her family's contribution to the city's growth in her 20 years as Chairman and CEO of Playboy Enterprises—a leadership term that made her the longest serving female CEO of a public company ever. After transforming the magazine company into a global multimedia and licensing company, she expanded her business interests and has remained a fixture at The Executives' Club and one of the city's most enthusiastic business advocates.

At Corn Products International, Gordon has enhanced the company's priority of supporting local charitable agencies and advancing cultural, civic, and humanitarian causes. Corn Products has also been named one of "America's Most Admired Companies" by *Fortune Magazine* for the last four years.

As for Keywell, he's used his success at Groupon as an avenue to advance the bold ideas of others—primarily as co-founder and Managing Partner of Lightbank. Deepening his community involvement, he is Chairman of the Illinois Innovation Council and, in answering a call to service from Mayor Rahm Emanuel, he serves on the Mayor's Committee on Technology Infrastructure and the Mayor's Chicago-China Friendship Initiative.

At the CEO Breakfast, Keywell compared the prominent nature of Chicago's Olympic

Mayor Richard M. Daley and his wife Maggie, and Patrick Ryan and his wife Shirley, have supported the mission of The Executives' Club in a variety of ways over the last two decades. In 2009, in the days after Chicago was denied its bid to host the 2016 Olympics, it was at The Club that Daley and Ryan expressed the intrinsic benefits and value of this ambitious pursuit.

Members and guests at the Chicago CEO Breakfast, "Leadership, Chicago-Style: Executive Insights on Competitiveness and Change," at the Fairmont Chicago, Millennium Park, volunteered their own questions to the morning's panelists through moderator Christie Hefner.

35

PwC

PwC helps organizations and individuals create the value they're looking for. We're a member of the PwC network of firms in 158 countries with close to 169,000 people committed to delivering quality in assurance, tax and advisory services. Bringing unique perspectives, skills and backgrounds, the people of PwC work closely with clients to deliver sustainable solutions tailored to address their unique business issues.

In maintaining client relationships across the globe, PwC and its people help promote Chicago as one of the world's leading business centers. The firm also carries on its enduring investment in the city and surrounding communities. "Our people are passionate about making a difference in the communities in which we work and live," said Vice Chairman, Client Service, Jay Henderson. "Our corporate responsibility programs facilitate our ability to make an impact."

Through its partnership with the United Way, its contributions through the PwC Charitable Foundation and its employee volunteer initiatives, PwC supports many worthwhile causes. The firm's primary charitable focus, however, is supporting youth education that provides growth opportunities for children, advances future leaders and develops the base of professionals who will be equipped to deal with an increasingly complex marketplace.

PwC gives its people unlimited paid time off to participate in firm sponsored volunteer initiatives. The firm also provides its people with 10 hours of paid time off to volunteer for causes of their choice. With more than 2,600 partners and staff, PwC's Greater Chicago team has led the US Firm in raising more than $1 million dollars annually for United Way for the last five consecutive years.

The firm's people are at the heart of PwC's commitment to clients and communities, and the key to its business success. Armed with tools that include enriching professional experiences, everyday coaching, timely and productive feedback and high-quality learning and development opportunities, PwC's teams work together to help clients respond to an increasingly complex regulatory environment and address today's accounting and financial reporting challenges, optimize operations through sustainable cost reduction and help deliver improvements in people, processes and technology.

PwC continues to expand its ability to help clients with high priority issues by bringing in new talent and resources, such as the acquisition of Diamond Management & Technology Consultants (a sponsor of The Executives' Club of Chicago's Centennial Celebration). Adam Gutstein, former president and CEO of Diamond and now a PwC Principal said, "PwC and Diamond were a great fit in terms of our culture and our ability to team with our clients. You

Through its partnership with the United Way, its contributions through the PwC Charitable Foundation and its employee volunteer initiatives, PwC supports many worthwhile causes.

need to have high quality work and high quality relationships. We also share a commitment to community, both here in Chicago and beyond."

PwC continually challenges its professionals to adopt fresh thinking to generate innovative solutions to complex business issues through our Assurance, Tax, and Advisory teams. The firm's Innovation Office works to accelerate innovation by inspiring new ideas and reducing barriers to their implementation. PwC also facilitates crowd-sourcing of ideas with its people through an idea management platform, sponsors high-profile innovation campaigns and contests within the firm, and organizes collaboration opportunities with external organizations.

With a broad network of business experience and a cohesive focus on innovation and technology and a commitment to delivering the highest quality, PwC is poised to extend its success in building relationships that create value. "We pursue our potential by maintaining and developing new client relationships, attracting and investing in the very best people, expanding into new geographies, broadening our industry focus and refining our service lines," said Henderson. "This strategy has enabled us to deliver exceptional results for clients throughout our history, and we expect it will continue to serve us well going forward."

bid to the city's successful proposal to host the North Atlantic Treaty Organization (NATO) and G-8 summits in May of 2012. "We need to leverage our opportunities to showcase Chicago and what's going on here," he said. "The G-8 summit is one of those opportunities."

Whether it's a city or an entrepreneur, pursuing big plans means overcoming a fear of failure, according to Keywell. "Those who embrace risk often go on to do great things," he said, reminiscent of Mayor Daley's words on the risks and rewards of progress in 2009.

According to Ryan, the culture looked down on entrepreneurs when he was planting the seeds of Aon in the 1960s. "Back then, you were expected to get a job with a big company," he told the Chicago CEO Breakfast. "Today, the capital is there for new ventures and you can attract people of great talent who want to be part of building something."

A month before this momentous Chicago CEO Breakfast, Mayor Emanuel highlighted the city's growing entrepreneurial advantages in his special address to The Executives' Club. Carrying on the tradition of the office, the mayor outlined his administration's objectives in the coming years and asked the business community to invest in the city's economic future. "We are creating the conditions that create jobs," Emanuel said. "We are repairing our past, preparing for our future, and keeping an eye on where we are going."

At the start of an address titled, "The Future of Economic Development in Chicago," Mayor Emanuel announced that Dow Chemical would bring 400 new jobs to Chicago. In the course of a vigorous speech peppered with humor, he delved into the details of the city's budget, heralded the effort to improve the city's school system, and promoted the potential of a city that in 15 years is likely to become the first mega-city in North America. Citing Chicago's global footprint as a "crucial strategic advantage," he connected its future promise to those who shape its character. "This is a city that's going places," he said. "This is a city on the move. If we make decisions, if we make the tough calls, the families that make up this city will be rewarded."

A SUPPORT SYSTEM THAT PUTS CHALLENGES IN PERSPECTIVE

Succeeding a mayor who had, in his own right, become synonymous with the city's blend of authentic attributes certainly doesn't make an already demanding job any easier. Yet, Mayor Emanuel's comfort level with the city and the

Paul S. Otellini, President and CEO of Intel, addressed members and guests of The Executives' Club at its February 24, 2010 Global Leaders Luncheon.

public spotlight seems to suggest otherwise. In his first two mayoral appearances at The Executives' Club, Emanuel's rallying efforts against the impediments of a fragile economic recovery were emblematic of Daley's presence at The Club at the start of a new century.

By 2001, the deflating bubble that was the booming dot-com economy of the late 1990s touched off a wave of downsizing and business failures felt within The Club's membership. Rather than easing its interest in advancing technology, The Club launched its quarterly Technology Conferences to more formally explore the issues and opportunities of evolving technologies.

Reaffirming existing relationships and building new alliances with local, national and international organizations, The Club hosted the first Global Information Technology Summit in 2001. In opening the event, Mayor Daley welcomed the invited experts from Asia, Europe, and North and Latin America, and discussed Chicago's efforts to become a leading global center for high-tech businesses. In a keynote address, Microsoft CEO Steve Ballmer provided perspective on the larger landscape of technology and technology as an industry.

The terrorist strikes of September 11, 2001 shifted the nation's focus from economic issues to war and anti-terrorism efforts at home and around the world. As a setting that instilled a sense of community, The Club moved forward with a fall season that opened September 27th with an address by G. Richard Wagoner, Jr., President and CEO of General Motors at the time.

Chris Galvin, then Chairman & CEO of Motorola, was the featured speaker at a special luncheon and seminar a month later. In his address, Galvin detailed his company's

S&C's 47-acre Chicago facility (in foreground) has been instrumental to the company's growth into a global organization that proudly celebrates 100 years in business.

S&C ELECTRIC

For S&C Electric Company, celebrating its 100 years in business is an opportunity to recognize the thoughtful leadership and strategic ambition of an entrepreneurial past that continues to drive the company of today. "Throughout our company's history, we have followed the same guiding principles," said John W. Estey, President and Chief Executive Officer of S&C Electric Company in Chicago and Chairman of the Board and Chief Executive Officer of S&C's operations in Canada, China, Brazil, Mexico and Europe. "Founded on the commitment of maintaining rock solid integrity in all of our business dealings, we have always focused on the safety of our people and the quality of our products, and we have always taken a long-term view of our business. That those principles have endured for 100 years is a key ingredient to our success."

S&C's origins are tied to the birth of the electric power industry itself. Samuel Insull, Thomas Edison's personal secretary, established Commonwealth Edison and hired highly skilled engineers that included Edmund O. Schweitzer and Nicholas J. Conrad. While remaining at the utility, Schweitzer and Conrad created the first reliable high-voltage fuse. Their innovative device used a non-conductive fluid to quench the potentially destructive arc that results when a high-voltage circuit is interrupted. In 1911, the two inventors formed a company, Schweitzer & Conrad, to manufacture their pioneering "Liquid Fuse."

Schweitzer & Conrad ultimately became S&C Electric Company, and the Liquid Fuse was the first in a series of S&C innovations that helped revolutionize the delivery of electric power and turn the company into one of Chicago's leading manufacturers. Under John Conrad's leadership, which began in the mid-1940s, the company reinvested profits for the long term, a strategy that continues today.

It is behind the strength of its people that S&C, now an employee-owned company, has grown into a global organization with a worldwide workforce of more than 2,500 full-time employees supported by an array of in-house training programs. More than 300 members of the S&C team have been with the company 25 years or longer. "With individuals and communities depending on our products, it's important to have people who understand not just what they're doing, but why they're doing it," said Estey, who has held various leadership positions at S&C since 1972. "As we celebrate the company's longevity we also celebrate the fact that we've been successful because we've had tremendous employee longevity." Reflecting the company's commitment to the lineage of its human capital, S&C's headquarters in Chicago's diverse and dynamic Rogers Park neighborhood is officially named the John R. Conrad Industrial Campus.

In its centennial year, the company's roster of customers continues to grow—from electric utilities to wind-farm and solar-power developers who rely on S&C's products and project management services in adapting to the fast-growing renewable-energy industry. In fact, with its recent introduction of IntelliTEAM® SG, the third generation of its automatic restoration system, S&C provides "distributed intelligence" on the electrical distribution grid. Combined with its award-winning IntelliRupter® and the company's sophisticated communications devices, IntelliTEAM SG is helping make the vision of a "smart" distribution grid a reality. "What we're doing today people wouldn't have dreamed we could do even ten years ago," said Estey.

The company's current research and development is enhanced by the S&C Advanced Technology Center (ATC), a one-of-a-kind testing laboratory that enables S&C to test prototypes of its innovative electrical products close to home instead of in labs outside the U.S.

Raising the hi-tech profile of Chicago and building on its support of the community through the S&C Foundation, the company's investment in its future still revolves around the ideals of its past. "S&C has called Chicago home for 100 years because this is a world-class city with world-class resources," said Estey. "Adding to the strengths that have fueled our success, we will continue to deliver solutions to customers here and around the globe for many years to come."

involvement in rescue efforts following the attacks on the World Trade Center. He spoke about technology and wireless communication's increased importance to security, noting that fingerprint detection from two-way radios and wireless baggage tags are no longer gadgets of the future but today's reality. Galvin also introduced an initiative Motorola created to support the nation's healing process. With the help of a multimedia presentation showing a powerful series of advertisements, he emphasized America's need to look ahead to better and brighter days. Other business leaders that filled out the speakers' schedule—including Anne Mulchahy, then Chairman and CEO of Xerox—echoed Galvin's unifying sentiments.

The Club also continued to reach out to other organizations and, in cooperation with the mayor's office, strengthened its ties with the World Economic Forum. With Mayor Daley, The Club secured the participation of Chicago business leaders at the Forum's annual meetings. The mayor and Maggie Daley also continued to attend receptions at The Club that, in welcoming foreign dignitaries to the city, enhanced Chicago's image as a global business center.

It was the synergy of its relationships with the business community and the mayor's team that prompted The Club to introduce the Women's Leadership Breakfast Series and establish the New Leaders Circle program and the New Leaders Board in 2004. When the market collapse of 2008 led to layoffs, dislocation and retrenchment in nearly all business sectors, The Club's support system and added programming pillars became even more important. Both the established and aspiring leaders who had come to rely on The Club as a key professional development and networking resource again recognized the value of the organization in troubled times.

"The idea of getting out of your office and going to The Club to listen to others who are also having challenges and issues has great value," said Carl Vander Wilt, retired Chairman and CEO of CenTrust Bank. Vander Wilt, who is also a former Chief Financial Officer of the Federal Reserve Bank of Chicago, is one of 46 CEOs and senior executives of top Chicago companies that make up The Club's Board of Directors. He has also been treasurer of The Club since 2006.

"By sharing in the conversations, understanding the issues, digesting it all and applying key takeaways to your own life or your own business situation, you are taking actions to improve your future," he said. "I think that makes the connections and opportunities that The Club provides even greater in a difficult economic environment than in an easier time."

It was with the slow economic recovery as a backdrop that The Executives' Club began preparing for its 2011 Centennial Celebration. As globally recognized leaders like Paul S. Otellini, President and CEO of Intel Corporation, and emerging Chicago-based business pioneers like Larry Kaplan, then CEO of NAVTEQ, graced the stage of The Club in 2010, the organization's management staff and committee members were planning a centennial season framed around four full-day summits addressing the audiences, industries, and markets likely to shape the economic future of the city and the nation.

By the time the curtain lifted on its first full-day centennial affair, the Women's Leadership Centennial Summit on March 25, 2011, Melissa Bean had become President and CEO of The Executives' Club, and a new era was underway.

Ellen Costello of BMO Harris Bank and John Daniels Jr., Firm Chairman at Quarles & Brady LLP, were among the guests at The Club's festive Holiday Reception held December 1, 2011 at The Northern Trust Company.

MAKING A COMMITMENT TO THE NEXT 100 YEARS

There aren't many organizations whose origins pre-date World War I, commercial air travel, and the ratification of four of the 50 states. Those that can reach back to the threads of such a deep history often do so not simply to celebrate longevity but to reaffirm their identity and better inform their future.

"A hundred years is a long time," said John W. Rowe, Chairman and CEO Exelon Corporation. "We see great institutions come and go, so an organization that has found service and supporters for a century is in fact a very important thing that should be both honored and celebrated." In fact, one of the earliest newsletters of The Club, dated December 25, 1925, lists among its newest members Louis A. Ferguson, Jr., a construction engineer at Commonwealth Edison Company.

Leading the parent company of ComEd, an energy provider with more than 100 years of experience, Rowe knows the relentless hurdles of long-term survival and the importance of service and value that differentiates an enterprise. "To use a modern phrase, The Executives' Club of Chicago is a form of continuing education," he said. "Through the speakers it presents, The Club gives individuals in the business community the chance to learn from industry leaders and, in some cases, political and government figures from outside the community. Through its networking opportunities, it offers members the unique chance to learn from each other."

As the head of another iconic Chicago-based company, one that has also reached the century mark in 2011, John Estey views the milestone with astute perspective as well. "No organization gets to celebrate a centennial by simply surviving," said Estey, President and CEO of S&C Electric Company. "You have to succeed, and that takes a lot of energy, enthusiasm, and a lot perseverance and adaptability. Nothing today is the way it was 100 years ago, so an organization really has to have changed and adapted to succeed. For The Executives' Club to have reached 100 years is a real testament to the fact that it has changed, it has stayed relevant, and it has answered the evolving needs of the business community. Over many decades, it has provided information that's useful and networking opportunities that help each individual member and each member company to succeed."

For S&C, its success has been supported by the benefits of membership. "To be in The Club with huge companies that have tremendous global success allows us to learn how they did it, what they did well, and what they wouldn't do if they did it again," said Estey, a member of The Clubs' Board of Directors. "It also gives us the opportunity to be able to help other companies who are still trying to achieve their global success."

The roots of BMO Harris go back well over 100 years, but it wasn't until Ellen Costello became President and CEO of the Chicago-based institution in 2006 that the bank joined the membership ranks of The Club. "For me, it was a great forum to meet a lot of other business

UNILEVER

For over 50 years The Alberto Culver Company has competed successfully in the beauty and personal care arena with some of the largest companies of the world. Founded in 1955 by Leonard Lavin, who with his wife Bernice guided its impressive growth from a one-product company into a global organization that has created some of the fastest growing brands in its field, Alberto Culver has become a $1.5 billion manufacturer and marketer with an additional portfolio of household products. The Lavin's daughter, Carol Lavin Bernick, now serves as the company's Executive Chairman and Mr. Lavin remains a director of the company.

From its headquarters in the Chicago suburb of Melrose Park, Alberto Culver is recognized for its entrepreneurial approach to bringing innovation and value to consumers and an excellent return to shareholders. Operating as a public company since 1961 and having been listed on the New York Stock Exchange since 1965, the company's success in keeping pace with some of the largest retailers in the world stems from its commitment to nurturing brands and people, values and ethics. It is now the fourth largest manufacturer of hair care products in the US and the second largest in the UK, and its leading hair care brands make the company the second-largest producer of hair care products for women of color in the world.

With its growth, Alberto Culver has expanded its support of organizations and issues involving healthcare, education, and women in the workforce and has established a comprehensive energy conservation effort dedicated to reducing the impact of its operations. The company's 2,700 employees, supported by a family-focused culture, continue to drive its growth and innovation across the globe.

Note: At publication date, Alberto Culver was acquired by Unilever, in May 2011, and the brands continue to thrive under the new corporate leadership.

leaders and to understand the issues of the city and the civic community," said Costello.

A frequent speaker at The Club and a member of its Board, Costello extended the involvement of BMO Harris to include its sponsorship of specific programs. "It's not hard to get a customer of ours interested in coming to one of The Club's breakfasts or luncheons because the topics are always very relevant, and the speakers are of high quality and high caliber," she said. "If I had to sum it up, I would say that the organization has always been forward-focused and always thinking about the needs of its constituents and its community. We see The Executives' Club as providing opportunities for our people to learn about other markets, to see the relevance of them. It's about staying connected and interacting with other business leaders, and there's no way that would be possible if The Club didn't create an environment and a set of programs and speakers that attract the business community. It just wouldn't happen."

It was more than 20 years ago that David Speer attended his first Executives' Club event. "It opened my eyes to a whole new part of Chicago," said Speer, Chairman and CEO of Illinois Tool Works (ITW), a company that celebrates its centennial anniversary in 2012. Speer's involvement with The Club over the years has included serving as a Board member and as its Chairman for a season.

Today, more than 10 ITW leaders gain advantages from The Club's programming. "With The Club's membership including small, medium, and large businesses and representing manufacturing, financial, accounting and many other industries, its diversity gives people a broad variety of topics to learn from and a wide range of people to connect with," he said. "When you add that to The Club's ability to attract global leaders and present global perspectives, it is a very rich forum for interchange that is fundamentally important to the life of Chicago."

As leaders like Rowe, Estey, Costello and Speer exemplify, The Executives' Club of Chicago continues to build on a heritage linking generations of the city's creative thinkers and doers. Paralleling Chicago's rise as a global city throughout the 20th century and presenting visionary business and government leaders from around the corner and around world, The Club carried its momentum into a new century of business that demands a global perspective.

Pushing forward, and boosted by the energy and experience of its new president, The Club's centennial year programming and presentations explored a spectrum of business issues—and each shed new light on the unfolding challenges and opportunities of the global economy. Under the chairmanships of Craig Donohue and David Nelms, the two seasons stitched together a year of connections and conversations that, indeed, pivoted around the needs and aspirations of the Chicago businesses community. From the seasonal forecasts of Savage and Swonk to the cerebral views of Lagarde, Immelt, Tilton, Ryan, Emanuel and many others, The Club delivered insight and interaction tailored to support success.

One hundred years after the founding group of businessmen began meeting at the Hotel Sherman, The Executives' Club of Chicago celebrated its past by, again, demonstrating its commitment to the future.

The Club's earliest group of members, pictured here, were an impressive blend of entrepreneurs, small business leaders, and industry pioneers. Among them were men who established enterprises that continue to thrive today.

THE EXECUTIVES' CLUB
OF CHICAGO
GLOBAL THINKERS AND DOERS SINCE 1911

A LETTER FROM THE PRESIDENT AND CEO

As we reflect on the one hundred year history of The Executives' Club of Chicago, our members, directors and staff should be proud. The same enthusiasm with which The Club's first members committed to building relationships, sharing best practices, and promoting Chicago area businesses is very much alive today.

In 1911, The Club's first membership roster of 45 businessmen included entrepreneurs such as Dr. Wallace C. Abbott, president and founder of Abbott Alkaloidal (now Abbott Labs), a company he started in 1888, at age 30. A practicing physician and drug store owner, Abbott's earliest innovation was forming the active part of a medicinal plant into tiny dosimetric granules—which successfully provided more consistent and effective dosages for patients.

Abbott wasn't alone. Other early Chicago business pioneers who came together to form The Club included CH Searle, President of G.D. Searle & Company (now a part of Pfizer), KK Bell of Calumet Baking Powder Company (now part of Kraft), and JJ Stokes of Marshall Field & Company (now Macy's). These visionaries built their companies into the industry leaders and large employers that are still widely recognized today. Together, they have been part of the fabric of Chicago's economic engine.

The contributions of our current members and directors to this city remain invaluable—and they now include women. So, as we recognize the foresight and achievements of our earliest members, one hundred years from now, Chicago will likely reflect on distinguished business leaders like Ilene Gordon of Corn Products International, Deb DeHaas of Deloitte, and Irene Rosenfeld of Kraft, as well as Greg Brown of Motorola Solutions, Craig Donohue of the CME Group, Bob Parkinson of Baxter, David Nelms of Discover Financial Services and others, and recognize how these members of The Club worked with Mayor Rahm Emanuel to enhance and advance this great city.

With this book, The Executives' Club celebrates the City of Chicago and the collective vision and work ethic of those who continue to evolve and strengthen its dynamic economy. We remain committed to our mission of bringing together Chicago's "best in class" business, civic and academic leaders with global thought leaders toward mutual success for the next hundred years.

Thank you all for your support and personal participation.

Respectfully,

Melissa L. Bean
President & Chief Executive Officer

In leading The Executives' Club of Chicago beyond the milestone of its centennial anniversary, Melissa Bean finds inspiration in those who have contributed to its successful past and those who remain dedicated to the promise of the future.

OUR STAFF

Melissa L. Bean
President & CEO

Daniel Britt
Global Accounts Manager

Deirdra "Dee" Crye
Executive Assistant to Melissa Bean

Jim Cunningham
Program Coordinator

Becca Dickson
Membership Assistant

Michelle Egner
Senior Program Manager

Elizabeth Ferruelo
Senior Program Manager

Kathryn Krivy
Vice President,
Program Development
& Board Relations

Mary MacLaren
Executive Director

Lauren Hammond-Martin
Marketing & Communications
Coordinator

Audrey Newsom
Program Coordinator

Colleen Pastuovic
Account Development

Rebecca Reid
Membership Manager

Scott Sarrels
IT Support Specialist

Gabrielle Saylor
Global Accounts Manager

Cindy Diehl Yang
Vice President, Operations

BOARD OF DIRECTORS

EXECUTIVE COMMITTEE

BOARD OF DIRECTORS

DIRECTORS

Gail K. Boudreaux
President, United Healthcare

Gregory Q. Brown
Chairman & Chief Executive Officer, Motorola Solutions

Greg C. Case
President & Chief Executive Officer, Aon Corporation

Ellen Costello
CEO & U.S. Country Head, BMO Financial Corp.

Chris Curtis
President & Chief Executive Officer, Schneider Electric North America

William J. Doyle
President & Chief Executive Officer, PotashCorp

Craig J. Duchossois
Chief Executive Officer, The Duchossois Group

Ana Dutra
Chief Executive Officer, Leadership & Talent Consulting, Korn/Ferry International

Colin Dyer
President & Chief Executive Officer, Jones Lang LaSalle

John W. Estey
President & Chief Executive Officer, S&C Electric Company

John R. Ettelson
President & Chief Executive Officer, William Blair & Company, L.L.C.

David W. Fox, Jr.
Vice Chairman, JPMorgan

J. Erik Fyrwald
President, Ecolab Inc.

Adam J. Gutstein
Diamond Advisory Services Leader

Paul A. Laudicina
Chairman of the Board & Managing Officer, A.T. Kearney

Aylwin B. Lewis
President & Chief Executive Officer, Potbelly Sandwich Works

Connie L. Lindsey
Executive Vice President, Corporate Social Responsibility, Northern Trust

Robert L. Parkinson
Chairman & Chief Executive Officer,
Baxter International Inc.

Tonise Paul
President & Chief Executive Officer,
Energy BBDO

P. Cody Phipps
President & Chief Executive Officer,
United Stationers Inc.

Anne R. Pramaggiore
President & Chief Operating Officer,
ComEd

Richard S. Price
Chairman & Chief Executive Officer,
Mesirow Financial Holdings, Inc.

Thomas J. Quinlan, III
President & Chief Executive Officer,
RR Donnelley

W. Robert Reum
Chairman,
President & Chief Executive Officer,
Amsted Industries

Tom E. Richards
President & CEO, CDW Corporation

Larry D. Richman
President & CEO,
The PrivateBank and PrivateBancorp

Thomas Ricketts
Chief Executive Officer,
Incapital, LLC
and Executive Chairman,
Chicago Cubs

Manny Sanchez
Founder & Managing Partner,
Sanchez Daniels & Hoffman LLP

Gregg Sherrill
Chairman & Chief Executive Officer,
Tenneco Inc.

Martin P. Slark
Vice Chairman & Chief Executive Officer,
Molex Incorporated

Donald G. Southwell
Chairman & Chief Executive Officer,
Kemper Corporation

David P. Storch
Chairman & Chief Executive Officer,
AAR CORP.

Scott C. Swanson
President & Chief Executive Officer,
RBS Citizens

CORPORATE MEMBERS

A.T. Kearney

ATKearney

AAR Corp.

Accenture

accenture

Amadeus Americas

AMCOL International Corporation

American Airlines

American Express

Aon Corporation
Aon Hewitt

Argo, Inc.

Ariel Investments

CORPORATE MEMBERS

Arthur J. Gallagher

Aspen Marketing Services

Associated Bank

Atkore International

Bain & Company, Inc.

Baker & McKenzie International

Banco Popular

Bank of America

Baxter International Inc.

Blackwell Consulting Services

CORPORATE MEMBERS

Blake, Cassels & Graydon (US) LLP

Blue Cross and Blue Shield Association

Blue Cross Blue Shield of Illinois

BMO Harris Bank

BNP Paribas

Burson-Marsteller

Burwood Group, Inc.

Canright Communications

CANRIGHT

Career Education Corporation

CastleOak Securities, L.P.

CORPORATE MEMBERS

CORPORATE MEMBERS

CDW Corporation

CEDA

Charles Schwab

Chicago Board Options Exchange, Inc.

Chicago Cubs

Chicago United

CIMCO Communications

Cisco Systems, Inc.

Citadel LLC

CITYTECH, Inc.

CORPORATE MEMBERS

CORPORATE MEMBERS

CME Group

Comcast

Corn Products International

Crowe Horwath LLP

CSC

Culloton Strategies, LLC

Deloitte LLP

DeVry Inc.

Discover Financial Services, Inc.

Dover Corporation

CORPORATE MEMBERS

Draftfcb

DRAFTFCB

Dunn Solutions Group, Inc.

DunnSolutionsGroup

E-Cycle

Edelman

Energy BBDO

ENERGY BBDO

Entertainment Cruises

Etihad Airways

Euro RSCG Chicago

Exelon Corporation

Fifth Third Bank

CORPORATE MEMBERS

Fleishman-Hillard

Forsythe

GA Communication Group

GE

Girl Scouts of Greater Chicago and Northwest Indiana

Golden Apple Foundation

Golin Harris

GTI (Gas Technology Institute)

Hilton Chicago

HSBC - North America

CORPORATE MEMBERS

Humana

Illinois Institute of Technology—
Stuart School of Business

Integrys

ITW

Ivan Carlson & Associates

JBT Corporation

Jones Lang LaSalle

JPMorgan Chase & Co.

JPMORGAN CHASE & CO.

Kemper Corporation

Ketchum

CORPORATE MEMBERS

Korn/Ferry International

KPMG LLP

Kroll

Lawson Products, Inc.

Lee Hecht Harrison

LEE HECHT
HARRISON

Marshall, Gerstein & Borun LLP

McDonald's Corporation

McKissack & McKissack Midwest, Inc

Mesirow Financial

Microsoft Corporation

CORPORATE MEMBERS

Mid American Group, Inc.

MID AMERICAN GROUP
THE LEADING EDGE

Molex Inc.

molex

Morgan Services, Inc.

Nalco Company

Navistar International Corporation

NAVISTAR

NAVTEQ

NAVTEQ

NBC 5 Chicago, WMAQ-TV

NES Rentals

Northern Trust Corporation

Northwestern Memorial HealthCare

CORPORATE MEMBERS

Orbitz Worldwide

Pivot Design, Inc.

upisəpivot

Plante & Moran, PLLC

PNC Bank

PotashCorp

Potbelly Sandwich Works LLC

Powerful Methods Inc.

PR Newswire

PricewaterhouseCoopers

Pronto Progress

CORPORATE MEMBERS

Protection Resources International LLC

PSC Group, LLC

Quarles & Brady LLP

RBS Citizens

RCP Advisors LLC

Related Midwest

Roland Berger Strategy Consultants

Roosevelt University

S&C Electric Company

Safeway Insurance Group

CORPORATE MEMBERS

SALO Project

SÁLO | Project Search

Sanchez, Daniels & Hoffman, LLP

Sard Verbinnen & Co.

SARD VERBINNEN & CO
NEW YORK | CHICAGO | SAN FRANCISCO | LOS ANGELES

Schneider Electric

Scottish Development International

Segall Bryant & Hamill

SFP

Shields Meneley Partners

Siebert Brandford Shank & Co. LLC

Siemens Corporation

CORPORATE MEMBERS

Skadden, Arps, Slate, Meagher, Flom LLP

Skidmore, Owings & Merrill LLP

SOM

Sound Investment

Stax Inc.

SXC Health Solutions, Inc.

Tatum

Tenneco Inc.

The Allstate Corporation

The Boeing Company

The History Factory

CORPORATE MEMBERS

The Huntington National Bank

The NASDAQ Stock Market

The Nielsen Company

The Ritz-Carlton Chicago

The Salem Group

Tishman Speyer

TISHMAN SPEYER

Towers Watson

U.S. Bank

U.S. Equities Realty, Inc.

Underwriters Laboratories Inc.

CORPORATE MEMBERS

Unilever

United Airlines, Inc.

United Stationers Inc.

UnitedHealthcare

USG Corporation

Vela Insurance Services, LLC

Wall Street Journal

THE WALL STREET JOURNAL.

William Blair & Company, LLC

Wozniak Industries, Inc.

Xerox Corporation

CORPORATE MEMBERS

Amsted Industries

CGN & Associates

Chicago Convention and Tourism Bureau

Clerestory Consulting, LLC

Credit Suisse Securities (USA) LLC

Daugherty Business Solutions

DePaul University

Dyson

ECD Company

Electronic Knowledge Interchange

EMBREE FINANCIAL Group

Friedman Properties Ltd.

Goldwind USA, Inc.

Grant Thornton LLP

Graycor

Henry Crown and Company

Hitachi Consulting

JETRO Chicago (Japan External Trade Organization)

Micro Focus, LLC

National Industries for the Blind

PointBridge

RTS Realtime Systems Inc

Sun-Times Media

Telephone and Data Systems, Inc.

The Duchossois Group, Inc.

The PrivateBank

TradingPartners

UNIVERSITY OF
ILLINOIS AT CHICAGO

SPECIAL THANKS

The production of this book would not have been possible without the extraordinary support of our board, sponsors and membership. We'd also like to acknowledge the insights and efforts of a number of dedicated people. To bring the story of The Club to life in this book, Chicago writer Dave Whitaker covered the events and activities of our centennial year and delved into our deep history. We thank Dave as well as the design team at Pivot Design—particularly Samira Selod, Senior Designer & Project Manager—for their commitment and creativity. We also thank RR Donnelley for the generosity and expertise that allowed this book to be published in the city The Club has been honored to serve for so long.

While the historical images that appear in the book are part of The Club's archival material, the talented team at Joe Gallo Photography is responsible for the many present day photographs. Thank you to Joe Gallo, Emily Cikanek, and Yvette Marie Dostatni for capturing the best of The Executives' Club of Chicago in our centennial year.

We offer a sincere thank you to the entire staff of The Executives' Club of Chicago—especially Lauren Hammond-Martin, Marketing & Communications Coordinator—for their tireless help in coördinating interviews, gathering organizational material, and supporting the production process. We also thank the many members of The Club who offered their input and perspective through interviews conducted for the book.